CHAP

Also by Ram Gidoomal

Sari 'n' Chips

CHAPATIS FOR TEA

Reaching Your Hindu Neighbour:
A Practical Guide

RAM GIDOOMAL and MARGARET WARDELL

Highland Books
Guildford, Surrey

British Library Cataloguing-in-Publication Data. A catalogue record for this book is available from the British Library.

Published in the UK in 1994 by Highland, an imprint of Inter Publishing Service (IPS) Ltd, 59 Woodbridge Road, Guildford, Surrey GU1 4RF.

Typeset by the Electronic Book Factory Ltd, Fife.
Printed in the UK by HarperCollins Manufacturing, Glasgow.

ISBN: 1 897913 07 9

CONTENTS

ACKNOWLEDGEMENTS

Though there are books on Hinduism for the student and intellectual there is nothing in Britain for the Christian man or woman in the street who has Hindu neighbours and wants to share the love of Jesus with them. This book is an attempt to fill that gap.

Among the many who have helped in its production, special thanks must go to the Reverend Basil Scott whose encouragement sparked off the whole project. He helped in the planning of the book, read each chapter as it was produced and made numerous comments and suggestions. Thanks must also go to those who read the first draft and gave their opinions and advice. They include Dr Raju Abraham, Julia Cameron, Rupa Flynn, Professor Prabhu Guptara, Sheila Kanwal, Joan Millson, Sukesh Pabari, Shaylesh Raja, Sunil Raheja, Suneel Shivdasani and Robin Thomson.

Ram would like to thank Mike Fearon for help in various ways. Catherine Harwood gave invaluable help to Margaret in the production of the final manuscript.

Last but not least, Margaret would like to thank Hilary Warner in whose home most of the book was written. She provided a quiet atmosphere, relieved me of many domestic chores, supplied meals, and, as someone with a minimal knowledge of Hinduism, gave her reactions to each chapter as it came off the word processor.

We are glad that you have chosen to read this book and trust it will help you understand the background and outlook of your Hindu friends and neighbours. May it set you on the road to sharing the good news of Jesus with them.

FOREWORD

As Christians we all follow a faith which demands that we share the good news of Jesus Christ with our neighbours. That is a simple fact to understand but never easy to put into practice. It becomes even more complicated when our neighbours may not share a Christian background. They may be Moslems, Sikhs, Hindus or agnostic about religions. To understand their position, and seek to 'walk in their shoes' is never a simple matter.

Living in Britain today involves being part of a multi-cultural society. It is difficult to ignore this fact and fatal to sharing our Christian faith if we seek to resist it. The Apostle Paul appreciated the truth of this when he boldly affirmed, 'I become all things to all men, in order that I might win some'. His is an example that we all need to follow if we are to make a faithful witness for Christ in Britain today.

However, when confronted by faiths other than our own, this is never easy. Ignorance can be a tremendous handicap. That is where this book makes such an invaluable contribution to church life in Britain today.

Those from Asian backgrounds are making a significant impact on many spheres of national life. It is tragic to observe how reluctant the church has been to provide a model of integration for those from other cultures, who are now part of the British population.

Some churchmen have begun to recognise this problem. However, their solution lies in the pretence that faith is only a part of culture. This leads to the inevitable conclusion that as culture is a matter of background, so also are an individual's religious beliefs. Therefore each person should espouse their own faith – conversion is out of the question.

In this book Margaret and Ram have worked from a different perspective. They clearly separate faith from culture. Their argument is that Asian cultural distinctives are important, but that Asians need Christ as much as Anglo-Saxons! The encouragement they give is to seek to present Christ to Hindus without the unnecessary trappings of an alien Western culture.

What many of us need is greater tolerance for our ethnic distinctives while maintaining the conviction that Jesus is not the Western God. Here this book is invaluable. Clear guidelines are given as to how to cultivate relationships and mutual understanding with our Hindu neighbours. The concentration is on developing friendships and then taking God-given opportunities to explain the Christian faith.

The intention of the authors is that Christians might become culturally aware and evangelistically proficient at the same time. This is a natural conjunction, and their case is well argued. As a handbook for cross-cultural evangelism this little volume has rarely been bettered.

My first personal encounter with Hindu neighbours took place some twenty years ago while living in Wolverhampton. Next door lived an Asian family who were practising Hindus. The twin

daughters were in their late teens. Taking pity
on their neighbours, who loved Indian food, they
taught me the art of cooking an authentic curry.
That began a lifetime of Indian cookery. My children love Dad's family meals – especially the
Indian ones! I therefore have a great deal to be
thankful for. My Hindu neighbours gave me a real
gift by their tuition; whatever the finished product
tastes like, at least I knew how to do it properly!

I find this reflection disturbing. For I knew how
to explain about my relationship with Jesus Christ
in a way they could understand. They bridged
the cookery gap. I failed to share my faith in
an effective and life-changing manner. I cannot
help but conclude that Ram and Margaret's book
would have made a significant difference for me. A
blow-by-blow analysis of faith sharing to Hindus
would have been invaluable.

That is why I am thrilled to have the privilege
of writing this foreword. I deeply appreciate the
advantages of living in a multi-cultural society.
I deplore our failings as a church when it comes
to representing our faith to a mission field on our
doorstep.

May this book awaken hope, encourage action
and provide the means of enabling us all to share
the love of the Lord, who is changing our lives,
with those around us. Perhaps Heaven will record
the testimony of former Hindus who have met
Jesus because we had been able, by His Spirit
to introduce them to Him. In that case this book
will have fulfilled its purpose.

Clive Calver
London,
February 1994

PREFACE

During the last forty years people from the new Commonwealth have settled all over Britain. In this book we are concerned about those of South Asian background and Hindus in particular. We are using the term South Asian to include people from India, Pakistan and Bangladesh, as well as the descendants of those who emigrated from these countries earlier this century to East Africa, mainly Kenya and Uganda. To avoid repeated use of the clumsy phrase 'he or she', one or the other sex is referred to in different chapters. Where your particular contact is of the opposite sex, make the appropriate mental adjustment.

The book attempts to help Christians learn something of Hindu culture and beliefs, and to give some guidance on witnessing. The first two chapters set the scene and suggest ways of making friends with Hindus. Chapters Three to Six outline the basic beliefs and practices of Hinduism. Chapter Seven deals with the Hindu scriptures. Few Hindus are familiar with all of these. You may only want to read what is relevant for your conversations with particular individuals. Chapter Eight gives some details about the main sects of Hinduism. If you are touch with any of their members consult the relevant paragraphs. Chapter Nine describes ways Hindus have adapted to life in Britain. The remainder, chapters Ten to Fourteen, talk about sharing the Christian faith with Hindus.

Mere reading of the text will be of little value unless you get involved with Hindus on an individual basis. **Things To Do**, at the end of each chapter, are vital parts of the book and should help you to make personal contacts. Read the chapters in an unhurried way and act on as many of the **Things To Do** as possible. It would be ideal to work through the book in a group, discussing the matters raised and encouraging one another to act on some of the suggestions. Next time you meet you can report back on how you put them into practice.

No one who reads this book should assume that it says everything there is to say about Hinduism. Hindu philosophy is complex and the product of oriental ways of thinking. Most Westerners find it hard to understand. In addition, the beliefs and practices of Hinduism vary widely in different parts of India, as well as overseas. We have attempted to present, as simply as possible, some of the basic tenets of the faith and the most helpful ways of witnessing to Hindus. If anyone wants to explore the topic more deeply they should refer to the book list at the back of the book. But even this includes only books of a non-academic nature. If you want to read something about the more intricate philosophy and practices of Hinduism your local library may be able to help.

Throughout the book people's names are introduced to illustrate specific situations. The situations are real, but the names have been changed.

INTRODUCTION

Christians often feel they can't talk to Hindus until they have learnt enough about Hinduism. But when you want to learn to swim you wouldn't dream of saying, 'I won't go into the water until I've learnt all there is to know about swimming'! You enter the water and splash about, learning to swim as you do so. Standing on the side will not get you anywhere.

We would like to see Christians getting into conversations and building friendships with Hindus so that they gradually learn more about Hindu beliefs and practices through experience. This is why we have written this book. But when entering a swimming-pool for the first time you don't start by plunging into the deep end from the highest diving-board. You climb down the steps into the shallow end where you hope to learn to swim. There you gain confidence before venturing out of your depth. In the same way you can begin with a tentative paddle in the shallow end of Christian-Hindu relationships. Only as you build up confidence need you move into deeper water.

Hinduism is a major world faith practised by 13 per cent[1] of the earth's population yet few

Westerners understand it. This is surprising as
about 18 million South Asians now live outside
South Asia, many of them Hindus. The 1991 census indicated that there were a total of 1,573,935
Asians in England and Wales, most of them within
a corridor stretching north west from London,
through Leicester, Birmingham, Bradford, Leeds
and Manchester. 58.15 per cent hailed from India,
32.34 per cent from Pakistan and 10.51 per cent
from Bangladesh. See the map opposite.

Estimates of the number of Hindus in Britain
varies. South Asian Concern estimates it at about
600,000 in 1992.[3] Many of them are from Gujarat,
a state on the west coast of India, and also from
the Punjab in the north. Many of the Gujaratis
have migrated here from East Africa. Smaller
numbers have come from other areas of India.
Recently a number of Tamils from Sri Lanka
have arrived in Britain, fleeing from the violence
in that country. A small number of Hindus come
from different areas of South-East Asia, such as
Malaysia, Singapore and Fiji. Most younger Hindus were born in Britain and are British citizens
by birth. Many of them have never visited the
country of their parents' origin. The term 'British
Hindu' can be used to denote both their national
and cultural background.

Hindus who migrated to Britain usually established themselves in cities, where others from
their own home area were already living. This was
natural as such people spoke the same language,
probably Gujarati, Punjabi, Hindi or Tamil. The
largest number settled in Greater London and in
the Midlands in such cities as Leicester, Coventry,
Wolverhampton and Birmingham. Others found

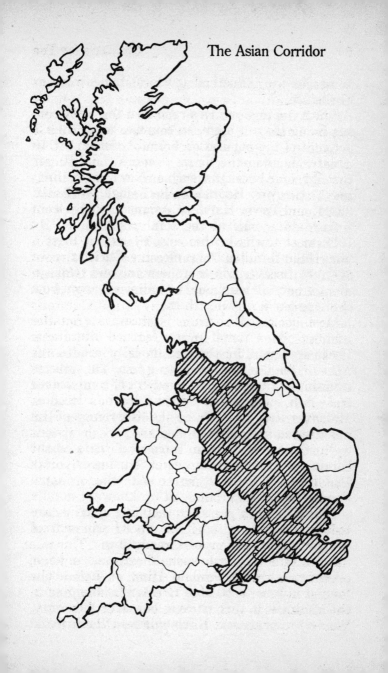

The Asian Corridor

homes in the industrial towns of Lancashire or
Yorkshire.

South Asian Concern's report on the 1991 census found that in eighteen counties more than 1
per cent of the population are of Asian origin. In
Greater London the figure is more than 10 per
cent. In some boroughs, such as Newham, Ealing,
Brent, Harrow, Hounslow, Redbridge, Waltham
Forest and Tower Hamlets, Asians make up from
a third to a half of the total population[3]. By
1992 most towns in this country had at least a
few Hindu families. As professing Christians we
ought to discover how to understand and relate to
them. Above all we should be concerned about how
to share our faith with them.

Most books on Hinduism concentrate on the
abstract ideas found in its learned literature.
These are useful for the academically minded but
difficult for the rest of us to grasp. The precise
meaning of these ideas is a subject of complicated
and often bitter debate among learned Hindus.
Moreover they are outside the experience of the
Hindus you are likely to meet.

Christians who have learned a little about
Hinduism often find themselves focusing on points
which are of little importance to the ordinary
Hindu. Such Christians end up knowing details
of which 95 per cent of practising Hindus are
ignorant, while missing out on 95 per cent of
matters that are of crucial importance.

Christians who are keen to witness to their
Hindu neighbours need to know enough about
their practices to be able to relate to them sym-
pathetically. If this is your objective you must
focus on information which will help you to build

bridges of friendship. Pray for the right opportunities to share the gospel with them rather
than trying to acquire academic information. Too
much know-how may distance you from most
Hindus and make it difficult to build meaningful
relationships. Although they enjoy intellectual
debate, this can usually lead the average Christian round in circles. It does not generally lead
to any worthwhile study of the unique claims of
Christ.

Hinduism is predominantly a life-style religion,
which absorbs beliefs and practices from the culture in which it finds itself. Hindus may also adopt
facets of other religions that appeal to them. For
instance, only 15 per cent of India's population
are Muslim yet Sufism, a mystical form of Islam,
is popular with many non-Muslims. Sikhism is
practised mainly by people from the Punjab, but
also has an influence on South Asians who practise other faiths. Chandra's family, though Hindu,
revered the Sikh holy book, the Guru Granth. If
you want to study Islam you will find many helpful
books available, and we are currently preparing a
book on Sikhism.

Hinduism has no room for any person or belief
that claims to be unique, so no human being can
easily persuade Hindus that Jesus is the only way
to God. It may seem therefore that any attempt to
approach them with the gospel is doomed to failure.
But such pessimism reckons without the power of
the Holy Spirit. If we witness faithfully and pray
for our Hindu friends, the Holy Spirit will convince
them of the truth about Jesus in their inmost hearts.
The stories in this book of former Hindus who have
come to Christ illustrate this well.

There are up to 300 million 'gods' in Hinduism,
so it is a bewildering and complex faith, with many
fine distinctions and shades of meaning. So it is
useful to know the basic beliefs and they will
be explained in this book. But it is even more
important to be aware of the practical outworkings
of Hinduism in the lives of its followers in the
West.

To further complicate matters, no two Hindus,
even from the same community, will ever have
the same views on Hindu lifestyle. The variety can
be bewildering. In Chandra's family, for example,
the colour red is prohibited whereas in others it is
highly valued.

A number of Hindus in Britain came here from
Kenya. When their families first migrated there
from India they brought over their images and
pictures of Hindu gods and installed them in
their new homes. Chandra's family lived in a
15-bedroomed flat and were able to set aside
one large and prominent room as a Hindu shrine.
There they established a miniature temple where
the pictures and images of the gods gazed down
on the holy books that were kept below. Now that
they have migrated to Britain they do not have
such a large house but they have set aside one
room for worship just the same.

When you come into contact with Hindus you
will notice first the outward aspects of their faith.
One obvious practice for some of them is touching
another's feet. Usually a young person does it to an
elder as a sign of respect. It can be almost a sign of
religious devotion, or it can be simply the equivalent of shaking someone's hand. Clearly saying 'I
worship you my father, so I touch your feet' has a

dangerous theological implication. But the action is often no more serious than, say, bowing to a member of the royal family. Some British people hug, and some don't; some kiss cheeks, others don't. In most cases touching feet is similarly a cultural issue, not a theological one. Shaking hands is not a common Hindu custom. When you visit a Hindu home, even if the man of the house shakes hands with you, you should only make a *namaste* to each woman in the family. This entails placing the hands together, slightly hollowed, and raising them to the breast or forehead.

Creative ways of reaching out to Hindus are important. Many Christians are frightened to do so; possibly because of fear of the unknown or of making fools of themselves. Streets filled with South Asian families can seem intimidating, but Hindus are just as human as you and me. Often they are more frightened of the Christian than vice versa. So take courage and step out in faith.

ONE

A CHRISTIAN RESPONSE TO THOSE OF OTHER FAITHS

A house in your road has been up for sale for several months, and now a 'sold' sign has appeared. You wonder what the new neighbours will be like. When they arrive you see they're Asian. Someone tells you they're Hindus. You feel at a disadvantage because you don't know anything about their culture or beliefs. You wonder how – or if – you'll get to know them.

How do Christians relate to Hindus around them? Christ's command is clear. He said, 'I have been given all authority in heaven and on earth. Go, then, to all peoples everywhere and make them my disciples ...' (Matthew 28: 18). We also read in Acts 4: 12 'Salvation is to be found through him alone; in all the world there is no one else whom God has given who can save us.'

Churches, in areas of Britain where there are large ethnic populations, are encouraging full-time evangelists to work among Asians. Mission agencies have set up home missions to assist them in this. For example, INTERSERVE, an organisation concerned with work in Asia and the Middle East, has set up Ministry among Asians in Britain (MAB). This places people, experienced in work amongst Asians, in areas of this country where they can help the churches. But a lone evangelist in a church can only reach personally a a few of those who need Christ. Organisations like South Asian Concern offer specialist training to equip those seeking to involve church members in reaching Asians. If fellow-church members become involved, the number of non-Christians who can be reached multiplies significantly.

But many in our multi-racial society today, even some Christians, criticise these initiatives. They ask such questions as, 'Is it valid to evangelise our Hindu population?' 'Is the Hindu really condemned because he or she is not a Christian?' 'Isn't salvation possible outside Christianity?'. We need to remind ourselves that the Bible tells us Jesus offers the only hope for all men and women.

Christians have often responded to the presence of Hindus in their area in five main ways, none of them helpful. Perhaps this book will help you work out more satisfactory means of getting to know them.

Some have ignored them

Sadly most Christians have chosen this way. Some because they fear the unknown. Some because they resent the changes which have been forced upon the area where they live. Others because they are racially prejudiced. A number have moved away when Asians came to live next door.

Some have attacked them

Racial prejudice has not been confined to those outside the church. Many white Christians assume,

sometimes without realising it, that being white
and British makes them superior. A Christian
from a Hindu background finds this extremely
hurtful. We may have heard some white people
say 'they' are taking over our jobs or our area and
'they should go back where they belong' – such
people fail to realise that the majority of Hindus
under the age of 30 were born in Britain. Some
Christians have talked about Asians in dispar-
aging and aggressive ways. Others have spread
gossip about things Asians are supposed to have
done. Even if they have never physically attacked
them they have often condoned those who do by
their silence.

Some have assumed that all ways lead to God

One white Christian said, 'They've got their own
religion. Surely we shouldn't interfere with it.'
Others are confused because they have heard
people say it doesn't matter which way you reach
God. As long as you practise sincerely what you
believe you will get there in the end, say some. And
if that's true what right have we to try and make
them change their religion? But this puts our own
beliefs in the place of God's eternal decrees. He
states in his word, 'There is one God, and there
is one who brings God and mankind together, the
man Christ Jesus, who gave himself to redeem all
mankind' (1 Timothy 2: 5). We must not place our
own opinions in the position of authority which can
only rightly be assumed by God's word.

Some believe Jesus is unique but that Christians shouldn't try to convert others to the same view

Such Christians believe that it is all right to talk to people of other faiths about beliefs they have in common. But they omit any part of the Christian message they think might cause offence. They are usually happy to join in inter-faith services where worship follows this pattern. They believe that we should only evangelise people who do not have any God. But if the early Christians had not witnessed to followers of other religions there might not be a Church today.

Some feel inadequate to approach Hindus

Some Christians are afraid to witness to Hindus because they think they don't know enough about their beliefs. Some fear their own faith may be shaken or 'tainted' if they get deeply involved with such people. They may also fear saying or doing things which will offend people of another culture.

None of the above reactions is satisfactory. The Bible is the only adequate guide to forming relationships with other people. Here are six main ways to do so.

Submit your relationships to God's commands

'Now God commands all [men] everywhere to turn away from their evil ways' (Acts 17: 30). He also

ordered his followers to take this message to the
whole world (Matthew 28: 16–20).

Love your neighbour

This theme runs throughout the Old and New
Testaments. Jesus commands us to love our neighbours as ourselves whatever their race, background or religion. He told the parable of the
Good Samaritan to illustrate this. Love is not just
having a warm feeling. It is practical. Chapter
2 gives examples of ways Christians can do as
Jesus said. The ultimate expression of Christian
love is telling one's neighbour about Jesus. Surely
we cannot be content to rest in the knowledge
that we have eternal life while letting the rest of
mankind drift into eternal death. We must share
with them the good news that we can know life
for ever in Jesus. If we truly love someone we
are eager to please them. God has *commanded* us
to love himself and our neighbour. We are being
disobedient if we do not do so. Jesus makes it clear
that love and obedience go hand in hand. 'If you
love me, you will obey my commandments' (John
14: 15).

Have respect for the Hindu

Sometimes we approach people of other backgrounds with preconceived ideas. Or we may
indulge in negative criticism when we observe
habits in them which are different from our own.

Such actions prevent us from making friends with them.

Read Acts 10: 1–41. Peter has his prejudice challenged head-on. When God told him to go and see Cornelius he replied that, as a Jew, he was not accustomed to mixing with Gentiles. He even told God that to do so was against Jewish law! He had not realised that the Christian faith was for everyone, Gentiles included. Many Western Christians have made the same mistake. They assume that the gospel is for the Western world, whereas it is for every human being; or that Britain is a 'Christian' country, when in fact few people here have any personal faith in the Lord Jesus Christ.

We must not relinquish our conviction that the Christian faith shows us the only true way to God and that other religions cannot save people. But neither must we assume that another person's religion is of no value. Cornelius was praying even before he met Peter. Most Hindus are familiar with prayer as he was. We may not agree with some aspects of their faith but to write off the whole of it for this reason may hurt them deeply.

Christians sometimes compare the best of what they know in Christianity with the worst features they see in Hinduism. Yet we are upset when a Hindu speaks only about the worst of what he sees in Christianity. Such an attitude is dishonest and unfair on either side. We must look for the best aspects of Hinduism; the reverence for God which it teaches, for example. Then we can ask ourselves how we might benefit from putting them into practice in our own lives. At the same time we should pray for ways to lovingly show Hindu friends the shortcomings of their faith. We need to respect Hindus but not the Hindu religion as a whole.

In all our contacts with Hindus we must take our cue from Scripture. Jesus treated every person as unique in God's sight. He was willing to lay down his life for us even though we had sinned and were 'far away from God's saving presence' (Romans 3: 23). We must imitate him in all our relationships with others whatever their origins or background.

Realise that religious systems don't save people

In this country many white people assume that going to church or practising other outward rites of Christianity will assure them of a place in heaven. Hinduism teaches that observing certain outward acts earns them salvation. The truth is that no amount of 'works', no religious rites, however carefully practised, save us. Only a personal faith in Jesus Christ as Lord and Saviour does this. The Bible speaks warmly of the openness to God of some individuals, like Naaman and Cornelius, who were not Jews or Christians. But it never commends other religions as alternative ways to God.

Remember that the gospel is for every human being

Peter makes it plain in Acts 4: 12 that 'salvation is found in no one else, for there is no other name under heaven given to men by which we must be saved' (NIV). Jesus died on the Cross to save all men and women. He rose from the dead to secure eternal life for them. And at Pentecost he sent the Holy Spirit for all who are willing to receive him. He helps us to do what pleases God. No one else in any other religion has done this. The Cross, the Resurrection and Pentecost are God's good news for all people.

If we only share the gospel with Christians and Europeans we are racist and, worse still, deny the Lordship of Christ over the whole of the human race. Either the gospel is true for all or it is not true at all. Through Adam's fall every human being was tainted with sin. All members of the human race need forgiveness before they can enter heaven. We are only sure of eternal life when we accept the fact that Jesus died for us personally and ask him to take control of our entire being. Only the Bible promises us this. Other holy books exhort their followers to try and lead a good life. They tell them that if they do they *may* be accepted by God. But they can never be certain. Only Christians have the assurance that when they die they will live with God for ever.

Rely on the Holy Spirit's power for witnessing

We should not let fear prevent us from talking about our faith. Even though we feel nervous we can still ask the Holy Spirit to enable us to say

the right things. Jesus said, 'Do not worry about
what you are going to say . . . For the words you
will speak will not be yours; they will come from
the Spirit of your Father speaking through you'
(Matthew 10: 19–20). We do not have to convince
people of the truth of the gospel. It is the Holy
Spirit who convinces and convicts. We need to
share what we know about Christ and leave the
rest to him. One person put it this way, 'With the
Holy Spirit we can speak even when afraid.'

If you observe these principles you will not go
far wrong in your relations with Hindus. Often
you can obtain all the information you need by
building friendships with them and asking them
questions. However this book will also help you
to learn about their faith and practices. Later, in
chapters ten to fourteen we will see in more detail
how they apply to sharing the gospel with them.

Things to do

1. Write down the name of any Hindu you know.
   Pray for him or her regularly.

2. Have you ever been in a Hindu home? If not,
   decide whom you could visit and ask God to
   show you an appropriate time to do so.

3. Visit a local Asian restaurant and sample some
   of the foods. You will then have something
   about which to comment and ask questions
   when you next meet your Asian contacts.

4. Visit the local Asian corner shop and get to
   know the shopkeeper and his family. Ask them

where they come from. Get them to tell you about their family background. It's important to know from which part of the Indian sub-continent they originate, as this will give you useful information about their lifestyle.

5. Make contact with local Asian Christians – the Christian agencies listed in the appendix will assist you with this. They will also be able to help you to get to know Hindus in your area.

TWO
MAKING HINDU FRIENDS

You cannot identify Hindus by casual observation. A person who looks South Asian may be Muslim, Hindu, Sikh or Christian. Though Hindu women wear saris, some Muslims and Christians do so too. Some Hindu women and most Hindu men wear European clothes. When you get to know them better you will find certain personal names common among Hindus. Some examples are Satya, Seeta and Devi for women and Ram, Krishna, Prakash and Chandra for men. So asking a South Asian his or her name may give you a clue to their religion. However, if you are still not sure, it is best to ask them. This avoids making a mistake which might upset them.

Though Christians and Hindus have different beliefs and different customs they also have much in common. Some Christians tell of happy relations with Hindu neighbours and work colleagues, but many are at a loss about how to form friendships. If this is how you feel this chapter should help to give you the confidence you need.

Hinduism has no founder, no creed and a variety of holy books, none of which claims final authority. It originated in India and the majority of its adherents (about 80 per cent of the population)

still live there. Though certain beliefs are common
to all Hindus in the country, other beliefs and
practices vary in different areas. Even within a
particular group no two people view or experience
their life or their faith in exactly the same way.
So no book can give you a neat package of the
doctrines and practices of Hindus. You will only
learn by personal observation.

The best way to share your faith meaningfully
with Hindus is by getting alongside individuals.
Try not to think of Hindus as a group of people who
are all alike. Habits we have perceived or heard
about in one or two are not necessarily character-
istic of all. The sooner you get to know particular
Hindus on a personal level the sooner you will find
out that every one of them is different.

We need to love our neighbours because Christ
commands us to do so. The Christian interpretation of a neighbour is anyone with whom we are
in contact. This is not part of Hindu teaching.
A Hindu's first duty is to his or her extended
family. This includes a whole network of aunts,
uncles, cousins, second cousins, relatives by marriage, etc. She will make immense sacrifices for
them and expect them to do the same for her. If
your Hindu next-door neighbour doesn't respond
to your overtures of friendship it may be that
she is too involved with her extended family to
make time for you. In that case develop closer ties
with other Hindus with whom you already have
contact. Having said that, this does not mean that
Hindus never care for their neighbours. Hindus
who have elderly white neighbours who live alone
are usually puzzled that they have no family with
them or near by. When Margaret first went to live

in an Asian area of London she found one Hindu
family had virtually adopted a widowed, white
next-door neighbour, as a sort of grandmother.
The children often came in to talk and sometimes
brought her Indian food to try. Occasionally their
mother came in to sit with the old lady, though
conversation was limited as neither of them knew
more than a few words of the other's language.

Many British people are not even sure they
want to be friends with Hindus. They prefer to
stay within their own culture and carry on living
as they have always done. But if a Christian
genuinely wants to live as Jesus did, she will
want to get to know Hindu neighbours and work
colleagues. The best way is to build up friendships
with one or two of them. This will help to break
down the social, cultural and religious barriers
between you.

Making contact

Before you can begin forming friendships with
Hindus you have to make contact in simple ways,
e. g. live in the same area, talk to Asian people at
work, take your recreation in places where they
do. If Hindus run a shop near your home, buy at
least some of your goods there. After being served
linger to talk to the assistant or other customers.

Jesus set a clear example in John chapter 4.
He was passing through Samaria and wanted to
share his message with some of its people, so he
did something very simple. He sat down by a well.
When a Samaritan woman came to draw water
he engaged her in conversation. If you read the

whole of the chapter you will discover that through this one simple contact many Samaritans came to believe.

Similarly you can think of ways to make contact today. As a woman walks down the street she might greet a Hindu neighbour who is sweeping her front path. Men, as Roger Hooker and Christopher Lamb suggest in *Love the Stranger*, can 'loiter with intent'[1] in shops, in coffee bars or round a pool table. When you get on a bus why not look for an empty seat next to an Asian of the same sex as yourself? If there is one, sit down and have a few words with her.

You may find that older men and women do not speak fluent English. But you could ask a Hindu neighbour to teach you to say good morning and good afternoon in the appropriate language. A word of caution here. In Asian society women do not talk to unrelated men casually. Much of what is shown in the media in this country gives Asians the impression that the moral standards of most white people are low. So if a white woman speaks to an Asian man he is likely to assume she is inviting a sexual advance. The same applies to white men approaching Asian women. So, especially early in a relationship, stick to conversation with your own sex.

Such casual meetings will not normally provide an opportunity for sharing the gospel. They are just a means of breaking the ice. You usually have to develop a relationship of trust before people of any race or religion are ready to talk about their deeper needs. Trust must be earned, so build up caring friendships with Hindus. You cannot do this with more than a few people. One

or two deep friendships will be more effective for
the Lord than many superficial ones. Such relationships will usually develop with neighbours,
work colleagues or people with whom you share
your leisure activities.

Leviticus 19: 33–34 tells us how God expects us
to treat those of a different background. 'Do not
ill treat foreigners who are living in your land.
Treat them as you would a fellow-Israelite, and
love them as you love yourselves. Remember that
you were once foreigners in the land of Egypt.'

Luke 2: 46–47 shows how Jesus went about
building relationships with people. 'On the third
day they (Jesus' parents) found him (Jesus) in the
Temple, sitting with the Jewish teachers, listening
to them and asking questions. All who heard him
were amazed at his intelligent answers.' First of
all he simply sat among the teachers. Then he
listened. Later he began to ask questions and
only lastly did he give answers. This is a useful
pattern for us to adopt.

Sitting among them

You may be nervous about how Hindu acquaintances view behaviour different from their own. If
you are in their home, do as they do, then you will
not cause offence. Elsewhere avoid commenting
if they act in unexpected ways. When you get
to know them better you can talk about the
differences between you and build up mutual
understanding. Obviously if you do not speak
the same language it is more difficult. However
you can express friendship in many ways without

using words; helping a Hindu neighbour with a carpentry job or his wife with a heavy load of shopping, for instance.

Hospitality ranks high in Asian culture. Accepting invitations to their home is the most likely way of finding opportunities to share the gospel. Asian people feel that when a person accepts their food it is a sign of accepting those who offer it. So when visiting a Hindu home don't refuse food or drink. When you are invited for a meal the hostess usually serves a cup of tea at once but the main meal not for an hour or two. During the interval the rest of the family will be keen to talk to you. When the food is served, eat what they put before you, even if you don't like it. You will hurt them if you refuse it.

You will, of course, want to invite them to your home in return. But you may find they keep on making excuses for not coming. This is because they are nervous about how they ought to behave. But you should keep on going to them. Don't feel uncomfortable about this. One Asian Christian from a Hindu background said, 'Don't feel obligated if they don't *ever* come to you. Continue going to them. They will be thrilled if you keep coming for ever.'

Listening

Beware of being so eager to share the gospel that you don't appreciate people's felt needs. Unless you sympathise with these and try to meet them if you can, they are unlikely to listen to what you say about your faith. Help them sacrificially. Be available when they need you. Spend time with

them. These are ways of showing that you love
them. When a neighbour is in hospital set aside
half an hour to visit her now and again. If you have
a car, and they don't, offer them a lift when they
need it. Offer your congratulations when a new
baby is born – and give a small present (clothes
are particularly acceptable).

If a Hindu friend is bereaved visit her as soon
as possible – in Hindu culture all acquaintances
do so. Women should dress sensitively and in pale
colours as Hindus wear white when in mourning.
Men should visit in the evening. Don't worry
about what to say. It is correct to sit in quiet
sympathy. You only need to touch the hand of
the bereaved gently on entering and leaving. Most
Hindus belong to an extended family and the
death of a cousin, in-law or any other relative is
deeply painful to them.

Remember that your Hindu friends are not
objects to be done good to. Such an attitude is
patronising and offensive. They are people with
whom you can share interests and heartaches.
Don't do all the talking or giving. They too have
much to give. Listen carefully when they tell
you about themselves, their background, their
family, their interests and so on. When you are
in trouble, confide in them. They have often suffered themselves and will usually be comforting
and supportive. Always accept gifts or invitations
they offer if you can.

Ask them to teach you a sentence or two of the
language they speak in their home – they will
appreciate your attempt to learn. And, if you
do so with enthusiasm, your efforts will pro-
voke friendly laughter on both sides. However

you will be wise to avoid making what seem to you humorous remarks, especially "leg pulling". Senses of humour are very different in different cultures and you may unwittingly hurt people.

Don't be so concerned with your own problems that you fail to appreciate that your Hindu friends have greater difficulties of adaptation than you do. The older generation feel foreigners in an alien culture. They usually continue to practise the customs and habits of their country of origin as far as they can. But as already pointed out most of those under 30 were born here. They tend to live with one foot in Asian culture at home and one in British culture at school or work. They are sometimes in conflict with older relatives about their behaviour and hopes for marriage or a career.

Making friends with Hindus should be only the beginning of your relationship with them. You should not only observe their customs and listen to what they say but try to understand why they act and think as they do. This will take time. In any case Asians do not hurry visiting, they engage in general conversation for some time before beginning to talk seriously. Listening is more important than talking yourself, it will help you to see things from their point of view. The more time you can spend in a Hindu home observing the way they treat each other, the pictures on the walls, the T.V. programmes or videos they watch, the more you will learn to understand them. As you listen to their conversation you will appreciate the way they think and feel. If they suggest showing you a video of an Indian film, do accept. You may not understand the language but watching it with them will help to build up friendship and trust. One way you may get Hindu friends to visit you is if *you* hire a video of an Indian film and invite them to watch it in your home. You probably don't know anything about Indian films but ask the manager of the video shop to suggest some titles. A golden oldie will be particularly appreciated. After you have established a good relationship you might show the film, *Jesus*. It is now available in Hindi. Gujarati and Punjabi versions are in the process of production.

Asking questions

Hindus are much less reluctant to talk about religion than most British people. They may well be the ones to start a discussion on such matters, but if they don't you should not be afraid to ask them about their faith, and then in return you can share something of yours. But do remember that the answers to your questions will vary according to whom you are speaking with and where their family roots are.

British Christians often worry about being able to remember and pronounce foreign sounding names. You may be able to ask children, who are usually at ease with English, to write down the name for you – then practise saying it at home. Children are very useful as interpreters, especially when there are language problems, but they can also explain many of the cultural practices of their elders. They too are learning to live in two cultures, so they will understand something of your difficulties.

Talking about our beliefs

This is a waste of time unless people want to hear about them. However eager you are to share your faith with Hindu friends it will mean little unless you show the love of Jesus by the way you treat them. As they observe that you care for them they may ask questions about your motivation. Then is the time to talk about the Lord.

Developing a friendship

Asian families are very close. If you invite Hindu friends to join you in an activity they will take it for granted that the whole family is included. They will appreciate your inviting their children to play with yours or suggesting a joint family outing of some sort. If the invitation includes a meal, avoid embarrassment by making sure it is vegetarian. Eggs may be taboo as well as meat; it depends on the family. So if you serve cake make sure it is not made with eggs. However, some Hindus do eat chicken or lamb, but never beef, because the cow is a sacred animal for Hindus. If you are unsure about what they do or do not eat, ask them when you issue the invitation. Punctuality is not so important in Asian culture as in British, so Hindu friends may turn up rather late for an activity to which you have invited them.

Don't be surprised if the wife talks of her husband as Mr ... rather than using his first name. This is considered the respectable way to talk to or about him in public. However young people who have grown up in Britain are often

keen to behave as their white contemporaries and
may use each others' first names. This can bring
them into conflict with the older generation.

Friendships at work may develop by being
involved in the same project, helping in a difficult job or just sitting beside a Hindu in the
canteen. If you are in a position of authority do
treat Asian employees just as you would someone
British. If an Asian fails to do a job satisfactorily
never imply that this is due to his colour, religion
or background.

We said in the introduction that a Hindu under
the age of 30 has probably been born in Britain.
Don't refer to India or East Africa as 'your country'
when talking to her. She is a British citizen by
birth. At the same time she may not readily
identify with Britain as her country either. Many
young Hindus, expected to behave as the older
generation of Asians do, at home, and as Westerners at school or work, are unsure about where
they really belong.

Above all remember the Lord's command to love
people (Leviticus 19:18) and speak as you would
wish them to do to you (Matthew 7:12). You will
not go far wrong if you observe these commands
and remember to pray for your Hindu contacts and
developing friendships.

Things to do

1. Ask a Hindu friend to teach you how to say
    'good morning' or 'how are you?' in the appro-
    priate Asian language. Start to use it regularly
    when you meet other Hindus. One warning,

make the phrase you want to learn quite clear,
otherwise she may teach you such greetings
as 'Hari Ram' or 'Hari Krishna'. These are
the names of Hindu gods and not suitable for
Christian use.

2. Invite a Hindu family to join you in watching
a video, visiting a museum or going with you
on an outing.

3. Another alternative is to take up Asian cookery
for yourself and to ask an Asian friend or neighbour to come round and give you a few tips.

4. Many Asian women love to sew and make their
own clothes. If you are a woman ask a Hindu
friend to go with you to choose a sari and then
help you to make a blouse to go with it. Asian
men are often keen on sports, like cricket or
Carum – a form of snooker.

5. Try to have a few Asian knick-knacks around
your house, so that your Asian visitors won't
feel intimidated by the Englishness of it all.
You may not like the effect yourself, but if you
really want to make your home seem friendly
this is one way to do so.

6. Try to befriend your contacts on their own
terms. They are not all the same. Find out
what they want to talk about and what they
like to do. Discover what difficulties they are
facing.

7. Contact South Asian Concern for a list of suitable videos to see with your Hindu friends.

THREE

BELIEFS COMMON TO MOST HINDUS

Introduction

The word Hindu comes from Sindhu the name of the region watered by the Indus River. Muslims, who invaded the region about AD 1200, applied it to the people they found there. (N B most of the Indus river is now in Pakistan.) However the Hindu religion goes back 5,000 years. 'Hinduism' is a term devised by foreigners. Hindus prefer to speak of their religion as 'sanatana dharma' which means 'The eternal teaching or law'.

Hinduism has no founder, no particular structure, no set creed. People born of Hindu parents usually regard themselves as Hindus even if they do not practise any religious rites.

The practice of Hinduism varies in different regions of India and in different sections of society in the same region. The origin of the name suggests that the common ingredient in it is the Indian origin of its followers. Hindus also hold a variety of beliefs. This makes it impossible to cover every aspect of the religion in one book. For example:

1. The vast majority believe in a supreme spirit, but some do not.

2. Some believe that respect for all living creatures demands they are vegetarian, others do not.

3. Some are devotees of one god, usually Shiva or Vishnu (pronounced Vishnoo), or one of Vishnu's incarnations. Others worship one of the goddesses. Most respect a number of gods and goddesses. But the individual Hindu may worship one god, a few, many or none at all.

4. They may express ultimate reality in personal or impersonal terms.

However there are some beliefs that are common to most Hindus:

The Ultimate Reality (Brahman)

Brahman is the term used for the ultimate cause of all things. It refers to the origin of all existence. He/it is not personal – but also not impersonal – the unknowable one. He/it has no attributes or characteristics, yet in the last resort is the only final reality. Everything except Brahman is illusion. Brahman is within all people and all things, a view of creation known as pantheism. This contrasts sharply with the Jewish and Christian view of creation which emphasises that God is separate from the world he has created.

The Gods

In normal daily life, a belief in Brahman alone is
difficult to maintain. Therefore ordinary people
revere one or more of the personal gods and goddesses. The most commonly worshipped are Shiva
and Vishnu. Most Hindus believe that Vishnu has
appeared on earth, at different periods, in ten avatars, or incarnations, to protect human beings. The
most well-known are Rama and Krishna who have
millions of devotees. Other gods include Hanuman,
the monkey god, or Ganesha (Ganaysha) who
is depicted as having a human body and an
elephant's head.

> Just as the ocean in the polar regions gets
> frozen into icebergs of a definite shape so
> Brahman can become apparently
> crystallized, and appear in any shape –
> human or animal, male or female, young
> or old. If you ask why God should bother to
> do this, the answer is that it is just for the
> sake of the devotees. In whatever shape you
> as a worshipper prefer to see Him or Her,
> in that shape God appears. As Lord Krishna
> says in the *Bhagavad Gita*: 'In whatever
> way men worship Me, in the same way I
> fulfil their desires.'[1]

Most Hindus worship the gods and goddesses in
the form of images made of wood, stone or metal, or
of pictures in their homes. Many will tell you they
are not worshipping the images but simply the
characteristics of Brahman which these represent.

However others wash and dress the image, feed it, put it to bed and so on, treating it as if it has a personality of its own.

Hindu gods and goddesses often combine within themselves both good and evil. Hindus believe that, 'all things have a good and evil aspect, depending on how you look at them. Time goes slowly if you are waiting for a train. It goes very fast if you're running to catch it.'[2]

Duty (dharma)

A Hindu's life is ruled by dharma. This refers to something much fuller than the usual English interpretation of 'duty'. It denotes a person's total way of life and conduct, including the duties which are essential for the support and protection of the individual, family and society. These change as a person grows older and passes through the various stages of life. (See Chapter Four.)

The eldest son looks after his parents in their old age because that is his dharma. When one of them dies he has the particular duty of making sure that his or her funeral is carried out correctly. Sons, sons-in-law and widow(er) all have specific duties to perform or dharma to meet. A son-in-law's duty is to look after the daughter. At the same time a second duty takes precedence over it. This is that the son-in-law is to be properly respected over and above the sons of the family. A married daughter is usually thought to be of little value to them. She is now the concern of her in-laws. But these attitudes do vary from family to family. The dowry system also often operates to the benefit of the son-in-law.

Works (karma)

Hindus believe that one has many lives. The type of existence into which a person is born depends on his actions in his previous life – these decide whether his next life will be a step up or a step down. Some Hindus believe that if they do something very bad in this life they will be punished by being born as an animal next time. This is called the law of karma which means 'works' or 'actions'. They should therefore be contented with whatever position they are in rather than complaining or being proud. Their situation is the result of the way they behaved in their previous life and so is their own responsibility.

Hindus do not believe that the gods judge them. Judgement is not needed because their karma decides their fate in their next life. However, despite this, most Hindus believe that the person who causes severe suffering will have to pay for it in his present life too. Human beings can tell the difference between right and wrong so it is up to them to do what is correct. There is no such thing as the grace of God to enable them to live a holy life, they have to rely on their own efforts to carry out all their duties, social and religious, in the best way they can. The acts they do must be appropriate to their caste (see Chapter Four). What is right for one person may be wrong for another. So there are no absolute moral standards in Hinduism. Good and evil are not determined for all time by a personal, moral God but by the structure of human society and most of all by the family.

Reincarnation (samsara)

Hindus believe the soul was never born and will never die. The soul in everything is the same. There is no difference between the soul of a plant or animal and the soul of a person. When the body dies, the same soul is reborn as another being in another place. This process is called the transmigration of the soul. 'Every living creature is a soul. It lives in a body and a mind, which it wears like clothes. "Just as a man when his coat is worn out throws it away, so," says the Gita, "do we discard this body again and take a new one."[3] Most Hindus also believe that the soul exists in inanimate objects. He/it is everywhere and in everything. Thus images are treated with extreme reverence.

A belief in reincarnation brings with it the possibility of many traumas that cannot be guessed at by someone unfamiliar with the concept. In his book *Death of a Guru*[4], Rabindranath Maharaj tells how, when his father died, he drew a circle round the house and sat in vigil for three days. He wanted to see into what form his holy and devout father would be reincarnated. He believed that the first form that crossed the circumference of the circle would indicate the form in which his father would return. He was shocked when it was

a bird. The family then started looking after birds,
thinking that one of them carried the soul of his
father. It was a tragic consequence of a particular
belief in reincarnation; though it also provided
a devastating challenge which eventually made
Maharaj review his beliefs and come to Christ.

Never tell a Hindu that he has not been born
again. He believes that he has because he has
been reincarnated. It is better to start from the
viewpoint of karma and talk about how he can be
released from the cycle of samsara. Tell him this
is not by re-birth but by a different kind of birth;
he can be born of the Spirit into a once and for all
new life.

Salvation (moksha)

Moksha is the way out of samsara when the soul
joins Brahman (the absolute). Every Hindu hopes
to achieve it one day. They believe moksha takes
place when the soul has become completely pure.
Then it goes back to being part of Brahman, which
is where it began. The round of births and deaths
is seen as a form of bondage. Many Hindus seek
the help of a spiritual teacher, or guru, to set them
on the right path. He teaches them to meditate
and practice yoga (p. 39 to p 42). The goal is to be
released from all deeds, both good and bad, and to
be absorbed into Brahman. But views vary about
what happens to them as individuals. Hindus have
no certainty about their eventual destiny, though
most believe moksha entails total destruction of
their personality, with everything lost, because
they cease to exist as an individual.

The positive side of this process is the calm and peace some Hindus seem to have. If you are in the right place, why strive for what was never intended for you in this particular life? The negative is the struggle to try and escape from the cycle of rebirths and attachment to the material world with its evil, grief and decay. There is also a tension between striving to earn merit and a belief in fate. Hindus believe they must work hard to earn a higher position in the next life (karma) but at the same time that their fate is decided by the gods.

The soul (atman)

As we have seen above, Hindus believe a person's soul is a spark of the divine essence which is never born and will never die.

Non-violence (ahimsa)

This is an important virtue for Hindus. They believe that all life is sacred. One must not kill anything: insects, fish, birds, animals or human beings. They have to give up every action which leads to the taking of life and they avoid eating all animal flesh. They also believe that animals have their own karma, or sin, which will be absorbed by eating their flesh. Thus most orthodox Hindus, especially Gujaratis, are vegetarians, though

some eat lamb when they shouldn't. Some will eat
battery eggs because they are infertile but shy
clear of those from free range hens because they
may have been fertilised and have the capacity
for life.

The non-violence principle is often taken to
extremes and combined with another one – destiny
or lekhio, meaning 'everything is written'. It is a
very fatalistic view of life. Hindus do not believe
in war, except wars of righteousness, which they
say are a different matter.

They believe the cow is sacred. This is probably because the white cow, the commonest sort
in India, is a symbol of the soul which is in
everything. Krishna is believed to have been a
cowherd. 80 per cent of India's people are rural
and depend on the cow for their livelihood. It
supplies milk, draws the plough and is often
used to draw up water from the well. Because
cows are sacred they are protected and in India
they wander where they like, even in towns and
cities.

For this reason Hindus are unlikely to eat
beef, even if they are not particularly religious
and eat other sorts of meat. When cooking, they
use different pans for clean (vegetarian) food and
unclean (meat) food. If they invite people for a
meal they may serve the meat and vegetables on
separate tables. In Britain, some Hindus, especially children, eat meat, even occasionally beef.
Even in families where foods containing meat or
eggs are not cooked in the kitchen, individuals do
sometimes bring them from the supermarket and
eat them in the house. This affects their ritual
purity (p. 67).

Paths to salvation (yogas)

Hindus believe that every person is responsible for finding their own way of deliverance from the wheel of existence. To help them do so they follow one of the paths which they call yogas. The word 'yoga' is from Sanskrit and means 'to bind together'. It teaches physical and mental disciplines which are believed to free the individual self from attachment to the world. The goal is the merging of the soul with the universal spirit.

The Hindu god Krishna said that whatever path a person chooses leads to himself. So a Hindu believes that all four yogas, and many other paths too, are equally valid ways of drawing near to God. Any Hindu god or guru is acceptable to Hindus, even though there are theological differences between the traditions they represent, which most Westerners find irreconcilable.

It is not offensive to a Hindu family for one of its members to follow a guru because it is not seen as breaking a cultural barrier and betraying the family. However if a Hindu becomes a Christian other Hindus will strongly oppose him, because it involves saying that Jesus Christ is the only way to God. They also fear he will reject the Hindu way of life and try to live like a Westerner.

There are 4 main yogas:

The yoga of knowledge (jnana)
This is the most difficult path. The follower needs a guru, or spiritual teacher, who can help him understand the complicated ideas expressed in

the holy books he has to study. One of the most
important ideas is that the things of earth – tables
and chairs, trees, animals, people – are 'unreal'
because they will not last for ever. This belief
is called maya or 'illusion'. Only Brahman, the
supreme spirit, actually exists, only those who recognise the spark of Brahman within themselves see
the difference between what is real and unreal. This
enables them to free themselves from attachment to
the material world and be absorbed into Brahman.

The yoga of good works (karma)
Hindus see doing work as making an offering to
the gods. A life full of selfless activity is the correct
way of using his god-given talents. By doing so
he acquires merit, and this ensures he moves
upwards in his next reincarnation. Better still,
the devotee must learn to act without any desire
for reward. Only in this way will he escape the law
of cause and effect (karma).

The yoga of devotion (bhakti)
This, the way of love, is the simplest and most
popular path for Hindus. The concept of Brahman
as the ultimate reality, without personality or
form, is difficult for the ordinary worshipper to
understand. A follower of bhakti therefore centres
his devotion on a god or goddess of his choice. He
uses an image of the god to help him concentrate
his thoughts.

This yoga does not demand knowledge of God
through books or meditation; it requires no specific rituals. The devotee only needs to have an
emotional awareness of God and to remember
him constantly. His goal is to be near God so that

eventually his spirit merges with the supreme spirit and is never reborn.

The yoga of mental exercise (hatha yoga)

This path is what many people in the West think of as being yoga – special positions and breathing exercises. Hindus use these exercises for clearing the mind which they believe helps them to find Brahman. Closely allied to Hatha yoga is Rajya yoga, which includes meditation and strict spiritual discipline. Hindus maintain that a successful follower of yoga can release hidden energy in his body, which enables him to control his mental and physical activities. Some believe it also strengthens their psychic powers, which in turn produces health, long life and peace of mind. They believe it leads to the freeing of the individual from the cycle of successive lives and his union with Brahman, the supreme spirit.

Since the second World War yoga has become popular in Britain as a form of physical exercise. Hatha yoga teaches that there are two currents in the body – one from the sun and one from the moon. They are at enmity with each other causing a person's mind and body to be restless. The yoga is designed to set a person free from them so that he can concentrate on his true self.

Even though people may claim they only practise the physical exercises of yoga, they are under the influence of their teacher. Most teachers are heavily influenced by Hindu philosophy and its goal of absorption into Brahman. They inevitably pass this on to their pupils. It also centres on oneself, emphasising self realisation, self fulfilment, self knowledge and even self salvation, rather

than salvation through Christ. It also teaches
that all religions are equally valid ways of discovering God. This conflicts with the Christian
teaching that salvation is found through Christ
alone. Therefore Christians should not be involved
in yoga.

Cautionary points

Not all the above beliefs and practices apply to
every Hindu. Hindus worship in many different
ways, in different types of temples; they are not
all alike. Reincarnation, the caste system, the
karma/dharma concept and the moksha concept
are the only ideas which are common to all Hindu
communities.

How, then, do Hindus know which gods and
goddesses to worship personally? They are born
into a family which honours particular deities
and they follow that family's customs. Though,
when a member of the family marries a woman
from another community, she brings with her the
gods she is used to worshipping and they are often
adopted by her new family.

A Hindu's beliefs are relevant to everyday life
in a variety of ways. For example, as soon as a
family member dies a Hindu engages in prayer
for the dead person's soul. He is worried about
its fate and there is no comfort. A lot of spiritual
activity and prayer takes place on the anniversary
of the death of a dearly loved family member. Try
to find out the dates and be prepared to pray for
the family at the same time, on your own.

Remember that Hindus believe that the souls

of the dead are reincarnated. Although this is directly contrary to Christian teaching, do not condemn their belief to their face while they are mourning. Use tact and avoid appearing insensitive to their grief.

Things to do

1. Read the chapter again and note any ways in which Hindu and Christian beliefs differ. Find Bible verses which explain the appropriate Christian beliefs.

2. As different Hindus practise their faith differently ask Hindu friends with whom you have a good relationship:

   a. What they believe about God.
   b. Which gods the family worships.
   c. What they believe about reincarnation.
   d. Whether they practise yoga or not.

3. Ask Hindus about the *character* of the gods they worship. Then be prepared to share about the character of God as revealed by Christ.

4. For a more detailed understanding of Hinduism read *Karma 'n' Chips*.

FOUR

CASTE, LIFE-CYCLE RITUALS AND STAGES OF LIFE

The caste system

As a student at college, Prakash remembers sitting next to two Indian students in the refectory. One announced in a friendly manner that he was from the brahmin class. The second said that he was a harijan – an untouchable. The brahmin winced. An embarrassed silence ensued.

They were all equals, sitting at a college lunch table in west London. The brahmin felt dreadful, immediately apologising. A British person listening would have been totally confused. What had happened that was so terrible? What is a brahmin? What is an outcaste? It's all part of the complex Hindu system.

For hundreds of years, Hindus have been divided into four groups called varnas. Their origin is uncertain. Gradually these divided into many smaller groups called castes or jatis. The jati you are in decides what job you do. Different castes are 'higher' or 'lower' than each other. The caste system does not allow inter-marriage or any social relationships

with other castes. You may not eat or drink with
someone of a lower caste or eat food prepared by
someone of a caste different from your own.

The 'highest' group in Hinduism are the brahmins
(not to be confused with Brahman). They were
originally the priests and are the Hindu equivalent of the Jewish priestly class. They tend
to keep the rules about caste more strictly than
other Hindus. In Britain, few brahmins have any
religious function though, in theory, any brahmin
male is entitled to become a priest. Typically, in
Britain, he will be a white collar worker. He will
come from a sufficiently affluent background not
to be a dustman or a cleaning operative. But he
probably won't be excessively rich either. Hindus
believe that they need to have been born into the
brahmin class, in their present lifetime, if they are
to stand any chance of immediate moksha at the
end of their present existence.

The next group were the kings, soldiers and aris-
tocrats. Then came the middle class merchants
and traders. The fourth group were the peasant
farmers and servants.

There were also many people engaged in what
were considered 'unclean' occupations such as tan-
ning leather (which meant touching dead animals),
sweeping the streets or cleaning toilets (which
meant coming into contact with human and animal
waste). They were excluded from the caste system
and known as outcastes or untouchables. If you
broke the rules of your caste you became untouchable. Caste Hindus used to put Christians in this
category. One Hindu who expressed interest in the
teachings of Jesus said, 'But I could never become
a Christian. They are outcaste people'. When India

became a secular state in 1950 untouchability was abolished by law but in practice the former outcastes still do the most menial tasks. However a minority have been able to secure a good education and a few have even become MPs.

Since the beginning of this century some caste barriers have been broken down in such matters as eating together and mixing socially, especially in the large cities in India. However caste is still important in relation to marriage, whether in India or overseas. Caste persists in Britain for this reason. Hindus believe marrying someone from your own caste strengthens the partnership. And they expect all young people to marry. As one woman said, '*Not* to be married is virtually unimaginable for a Hindu girl.' Usually only fellow caste members are invited to take part in religious ceremonies in the home.

In Britain, the caste system is difficult to maintain. Hindus work in factories next to people of other castes and eat together in the canteen, as well as meeting and sitting together when they worship. Over the last ten years even marrying outside one's caste is becoming more acceptable, though most Hindu families stay within it. On the other hand, some individual Hindus in Britain have their friends only from the same caste and even form social clubs to which they do not admit members of any other caste.

The life-cycle ceremonies

Before birth

There are several ceremonies. The most important parts of them are prayers to protect the mother and baby.

When Prakash's wife was expecting their first child they received a phone call from a member of their extended family saying that the stars indicated that a certain day was ill-omened. 'Be careful that your wife does not stitch on that day.' As Christians they ignored the advice. But it was typical of Hinduism. In many Hindu families it would have been heeded for fear that the wife might prick herself and harm the baby.

Birth

Astrology plays a major part in the life of most Hindus. When a baby is born, a priest will write its horoscope. This will be used throughout its life to find out the best times for important events to take place.

The naming ceremony

Hindus think choosing a child's name is very important because the right one will bring the child good luck. An astrologer may indicate that he hears a particular vowel sound which ought to be part of the baby's name. Families may also ask a priest to advise. They often use the names of gods and goddesses. Sometimes families in Britain write to ask relatives in India, especially the most senior male member, to give a name. In India, the ceremony takes place on the twelfth day but, in Britain, it may be delayed if the parents are waiting for family in India to reply.

The naming ceremony is simple but varies with the family or caste. One tradition is for the father to whisper into the baby's ear, 'Now your name is . . .'. The baby's family then give sweet food to

the friends and relatives who have attended the
ceremony.

The hair cutting ceremony

Other ceremonies happen during the early years
of a child's life. One of the most usual takes place
some time during the first three years when
he has his first haircut. Boys have their whole
head shaved and, in some families, girls too.
This symbolises the removing of any bad karma
from their previous life. Some parents living in
Britain take their children back to India for this
ceremony. It can be a useful point of contact
for a Christian trying to get alongside a Hindu
family. It is probably the closest ceremony to a
christening. Usually many relatives attend the
occasion. Whether you were present, or not, at
some appropriate time you can politely ask the
parents about its significance.

Being observant and asking for information
will enable you to pick up on the symbolism
of a number of the religious milestones in a
Hindu's life. Many of them, however, have lost
their religious significance as 'life landmarks'.
The symbolism is all that is left. In some families
they have a social, but no religious, significance;
some have abandoned them altogether; others
carry them out in secret; others perform them
openly. There is no standard practice.

The stages of life

Some time between a boy's seventh and twelfth
birthdays he is considered to have reached man-
hood. From then on he passes through four stages

of life. These used to be observed in India, but they
are largely disregarded in Britain.

The student age

For the three upper varnas this first stage begins
with the rite of the sacred thread. At the ceremony
the thread is usually slung over the candidate's
left shoulder and down to the right hip. In certain
families it is worn like a necklace and is sometimes
made of gold. Once a boy has received this, he
is thought to have become a man. He cannot be
married until he has received the sacred thread.
A man wears it through out his life, changing it at
festivals. A student's duties are to gain knowledge
by following a course of study, to show respect to
teachers and parents for their experience of life,
and to learn the rules and rituals of Hinduism.

The married householder

Hindus consider getting married and having children essential, in order to continue the family
and its social and religious traditions. Marriage
is arranged by a boy's or girl's parents – in most
cases even in Britain. Parents may ask the advice
of a priest or close friends of the family. They also
consult a couple's horoscopes to make sure they
are well-matched – and probably find someone
well respected as a go-between. Such people are
recognised in the community for their wisdom in
advising parents on the suitability of prospective
partners and their families. Unlike in the past,
parents usually allow the young people to meet
each other briefly and say whether they agree to
the match or not. Marriage signifies not just the
union of two young people but the beginning of a

relationship between the two families concerned.
A Hindu social worker in Coventry said, 'An
arranged marriage is stronger than a Western
marriage because it's not between two individuals
alone. It's between families.'[1]

Ram Gidoomal has looked at the pros and cons
of arranged marriages, the complex process of
arranging introductions and the dowry system in
his book, *Sari 'n' Chips*.

> In arranged marriages, the rule is that one
> marries – not simply another Asian – but
> a member of the same caste and the same
> community. Living in India, you can be
> spoiled for choice. But with Asians scattered
> throughout the world, it can be difficult for
> a family to locate a suitable partner within
> the same country, let alone the same town
> or the same street.[2]

Many Asians go to India where they may be
introduced to suitable partners from all over the
world. It is not unusual for an arranged marriage
to take place between Indians who have been
brought up on different continents. The Christian
who is sceptical about arranged marriages might
like to ponder whether the marriage of Adam and
Eve was a love match or an arranged marriage –
arranged by God.

Traditionally, the girl's family pay a dowry
which can vary from £100 to millions, depending on the wealth of the girl's parents or how
desperate they are for a suitor. The size of the
dowry can be a major source of discontent and
rifts within marriages, It requires delicate and

diplomatic negotiation as family honour and reputation are at stake. Trivial matters of protocol can cause immense ill-feeling.

A Hindu wedding ceremony lasts about three hours but the reception may go on for several days. Most brides wear red and gold but some now wear a white sari with a red headdress. However for certain families red is a taboo colour so a bride wears something else. The most important part of the ceremony comes when the bride and groom walk seven times round the sacred fire. After each round they stop and make promises to each other. The final promise makes the marriage binding and the girl now belongs to her husband's family.

A ceremonial fire is an important element at the wedding. In the 1970s when Chandra attended Hindu weddings in London hotels a tiny fire was lit in a metal bowl; but this was usually still enough to set off fire alarms! Now, special clearance is obtained. He remembers one hilarious occasion when this was forgotten. The fire triggered off the hotel's sprinkler system, spraying guests with water.

Strict Hindus do not accept divorce. They believe it is a disgrace to the families concerned. However, divorce is on the increase among second and third generation Hindus in Britain, just as in the rest of Western society.

The way of meditation
When a man retires he usually hands over the running of the family to his eldest son. He will live with his son's family and spend more time studying the holy books. In some cities in Britain retired people get together at the temple during

the day. Elderly people are highly respected in Indian society. The younger generations often ask them for advice; they have been brought up to do so. Most Asians are shocked at the idea of putting an elderly relative into an old people's home though here in Britain a few families are now doing so.

The way of renunciation

A few men in India give up all ties to worldly life after their retirement. These include their family and most of their belongings. They become wandering holy men, begging for food and spending most of their time in meditation. This stage is optional and not many enter it. It is not practised in Britain. However one Hindu woman in Britain said that though her husband would not enter this stage he accepted the philosophy of it and had adopted a very simple lifestyle.

A member of Preet's extended family who had lived a hard life did dissolve his assets, give the proceeds to his family and go off by himself. He disappeared without a trace until making contact five years later, from several thousand miles away. He had spent a period going around India, before surfacing in Europe.

Funerals

Though a family mourns the loss of a loved one they also look on death as a welcome release from life and rejoice that the deceased has one less rebirth to live through.

Mourning rites are quite elaborate. Anyone who has even a limited acquaintance with the deceased's family should visit them and mourn with them. (Consult Chapter Two for advice about how to behave.) The relatives usually show a great deal of emotion – they often weep loudly. Hindus feel it is a way of showing one's love for the deceased. To be restrained in one's grief is taken to mean that you did not really care for the dead person. In the days before the funeral the family are not expected to carry out normal household duties. Friends and neighbours bring in food for them.

Hindus cremate their dead. They believe that the deceased has completed his journey in the present life and will be reborn in a new body. They therefore burn, with the body, items that will be required in the person's next life, including food and money. Most families in Britain have the usual service at the crematorium. Be present if possible. Afterwards there may be a specifically Hindu ceremony where people pay respect to the gods. You do not need to attend this. But, if you can, go back to the house of the bereaved afterwards. They will appreciate it.

In India, Hindus build a funeral pyre (pile) – by one of the sacred rivers, if possible. If a senior member of the family has died the eldest son sets light to the fire. Prayers are said and readings from the holy books remind the mourners that everyone who dies will be reborn. The eldest male relative stays by the pyre until the fire is completely out. Then he collects the ashes. If there is a river nearby he will throw them into it. If not he may make a pilgrimage to a sacred place where he can do so. In Britain, ashes are often sent back to India for this purpose. If the relatives cannot do this they will go to some place

by the sea, take a boat about a mile out from shore
and throw them in because they say all holy rivers
finally mix with the sea. A person who attends a
funeral becomes 'unclean' and must have a bath
as soon as he gets home.

In the days that follow a funeral there are
several other ceremonies, the last being twelve
days afterwards.

Other sacred rites

There are many other occasions when sacred rites
have to be performed or the gods consulted about
some aspect of life. These will be carried out by
the local priest, usually at a shrine where offerings
of food and flowers will be made to the gods. In
Britain many families no longer observe all these
rites. Some rarely visit a temple except perhaps
at Diwali (see Chapter Six).

Things to do

1. If Hindu friends ask you to attend one of their
   ceremonies accept if possible, but don't partici-
   pate. They sometimes go on for several hours.
   Stay the full time if you can. You will learn a
   great deal that way.

2. Ask a Hindu friend to tell you why the life-cycle
   ceremonies are so important to her.

3. Ask a Hindu about her ways of mourning and
   expressing grief. Be prepared to share the
   Christian attitude as appropriate.

4. Invite a Hindu family you have visited to come to you in return. Remember their taboos when preparing food and drink. You may be wise to invite them the first time for just a cup of tea of coffee, but make sure you have *vegetarian* snacks available.

FIVE

HINDU PRAYER AND WORSHIP

No two Hindu families, especially in Britain, practise prayer and worship in the same way. Some observe every detail of the orthodox rituals. Others are quite lax. When you get to know a Hindu well you can ask him to tell you how he worships. Most of this chapter describes how a strict family does so.

Prayer, for a Hindu, does not mean the same as it does for a Christian. If we find ourselves talking with a Hindu about prayer we must establish straight away what we each mean by it. Otherwise we will be talking at cross purposes.

Most Hindus have no concept of prayer as a dialogue with God. But some do talk to him, asking for help or gifts and expecting answers, and some make vows. Kamlesh, who is now a Christian, remembers that he became very disheartened when God did not respond to his prayers.

However, Hindu prayer usually consists of reciting a short and formal ritual, called a mantra. This invokes certain spirits. There are different mantras with different spiritual meanings. Tone and intonation are important parts of the repetitious chanting. Other Hindu prayers consist of huge chunks of Sanskrit, a language related to the modern north Indian languages much as Latin relates to French, Spanish and Italian. These are recited by a priest. Intercessory prayers are also said by a priest, usually for a small payment.

Worship and prayer in Hinduism are of three kinds: essential ones, which happen every day, such as worshipping the family gods at the household shrine; those which are essential but only take place on special occasions, such as the annual festivals associated with various gods, or the thanksgivings which take place after some special happening in the family; and those which, though desirable, are optional, such as pilgrimages.

Worship at Home

A Hindu home usually includes a shrine containing a small metal or marble image or a picture, maybe just postcard size, of the god the family worships. Some flowers will be arranged before it. The shrine may be in a small room, in an alcove, or on a shelf fixed to the wall. In India it is often in the kitchen. This is convenient because strict purity is important in the preparation of food, especially that to be offered to images.

In Kamlesh's home, in the early hours of the day, they would wake the 'gods' by lighting a lamp, and singing mantras or chants. The mantras often begin with the sacred word 'om'. As he recites it the worshipper may put his hands together and lift them to his chest or forehead or kneel and touch the ground in front of the image with his forehead. Such actions show respect.

When the family rose they all gathered round the shrine. The holy books – for them the *Bhagavad Gita* and the *Guru Granth* – were opened up with great ritual. Other Hindu families might revere different holy books, but they usually begin the day with a similar ceremony.

Then the gods had to be washed and fed. This meant bathing the images in a milk solution every day and covering them with a special cloth. All the ladies of the household performed this task on a rota basis. In some homes worshippers anoint the image with ghee, touch it with coloured powders, hang garlands round it and offer it flowers or leaves. They burn incense in front of it and perform arati, the waving of lamps. In Kamlesh's house, a special solution, called tilak was made up and each idol and picture touched on the forehead with it each morning. This was a sign of worship and obedience.

Then the ladies would take turns to have a bath before approaching the shrine again. At a certain time each day, they would have another half hour of devotions when they sat and read from the holy books.

All food prepared in the home was first offered to the household gods before being distributed to the family and guests. Prasad, the food offered to the idols, was cooked in a particularly clean manner and dabbed around the mouth of the images or pictures of the gods. During the day members of the family might stop at the shrine to worship, offering flowers, incense and food to the image, or maybe spend half an hour before a meal reading from the holy books. At six o'clock they 'put the image to bed' after another special devotional time.

Hindu worship is known as puja, making offerings to the image. They usually keep the articles used for it on a small tray beside the shrine. These include red kum-kum powder, yellow turmeric powder, rice grains, flowers, fruit, an incense stick, sandalwood paste, water, milk, and a ghee-lamp. Ghee is clarified butter. Devotees of a particular god may perform a special sixteen-day puja at the annual festival of the god or goddess. Additional articles are needed for this.

When asked if he actually worshipped the image, one Hindu in Britain said, 'The images are more than photos or signposts pointing to God. They become what they represent'.[1] Another said,

> Only a priest can bring the living reality
> of the image into what would otherwise
> remain its dead form; and after he has done
> so, the image is treated with respect as a
> living being. So when we put the life in the
> idols, we can't keep it just as it is. Every
> day we have to give the food, we have to
> give the milk, and everything that a human
> might wish, every day.[2]

However Hindus vary greatly in their view of images. Some do not believe in worshipping them at all.

Sadly, in many Hindu homes worship stems from superstition rather than love or devotion to a particular god. The family fears that something terrible may happen if they do not placate them by performing the required rituals.

Om

This is a sacred symbol written in Sanskrit and is thought to contain all the secrets of the universe. It sounds as if spelt 'Aa oo m'. Hindus believe it to be the first sound through which the world came into being. Repeating it is said to give the worshipper control of his breath. As he breathes more deeply he mentally makes connection with God. Hindus always begin prayers, readings from the holy books and meditation with this sound. They believe it is a means of concentrating the mind and emptying it of everything else.

The Om Symbol

The Swastika

This is another good luck symbol which means 'It is well'. It generally signifies the keeping away of evil spirits and the promise of material blessings but its interpretation can differ widely. People

The Swastika

usually draw it in red. They use it on wedding invitations, decorative floor designs, in textile patterns and in various rituals.

What we think of in the West as being a swastika is the symbol used by Adolph Hitler. He revered it for his own purposes but actually used it with the arms bent in the opposite direction to those of the Hindu symbol.

Temple worship

Some Hindu temples are large and beautifully decorated, others small and simple. At least one priest will look after them, however small they are. He cares for the image and helps people to worship. In small temples Hindus pray on their own but in large ones a priest may be available to offer prayers for a group of people.

Typically it is not the whole community which pays for a priest or a temple, but the richest people. The idea of tithing is an alien concept to the Hindu.

In poorer communities, where there are no particularly rich Hindus, the temples lack any great decoration. There may perhaps be silver doors into the inner sanctuary, where the images are kept. The floor will be covered with a cloth on which the worshippers sit when they have removed their shoes. A small sum of money may be offered to the priest especially at weddings on which vast amounts of money are often spent.

Hindus consider it essential for a priest to give directions on how to perform particular rites. He has studied the religious books and his authority is respected. He conducts prayers several times a day, beginning in the early morning. Those who wish to, join him. He prepares the images, offers them fresh flowers, incense and food, which the worshippers then receive back as prasad (food that has been offered to and blessed by the god). Hindus also consult a priest about many aspects of life e. g. what day is suitable for opening a shop or buying a new car. He gives guidance about performing the life cycle rituals such as marriages, funerals, and hair cutting. The date and time of these are decided by horoscopes. Hindus may visit a temple once a day, once a week, once a month or only at festival times. Others may never go. There is no weekly holy day like Sunday. The most important rituals take place in the home. Visiting a temple is optional for a Hindu, but many in Britain like to go regularly because it has become the centre of social life for the local Hindu community. Older people visit it more naturally and frequently than the average Westerner visits a church. Perhaps as many as 80 per cent of all Hindus living outside South Asia, regularly attend a temple. However many teenagers and other Hindus born in Britain are not drawn to temples and this is another area that can lead to friction with their elders.

Congregational worship is not usual in Hinduism. But the morning and evening arati ceremony attracts devotees. Children learn to worship by observing what their elders do. Hindus normally visit a temple to view the image in the inner sanctum from the doorway. This viewing is called a darshan.

Worship usually has three parts.

Bhajan – hymn singing from the holy books.

Havan – offering fire to the god. The priest lights a fire on a special altar, using wood and ghee. As it burns the worshippers say prayers.

Arati – The priest waves a small tray containing five lights in front of the image. Then he takes it round to the worshippers. They hold their hands over the flames and then wipe them over their heads. They believe that by doing so they receive power and blessing from the god. They also sing special hymns and recite traditional prayers.

Before going into a temple the worshippers remove their shoes as a sign of respect. They usually bring gifts which they give to the priest. He takes them into the shrine room or places them before the main shrine to give them to the god. The gifts may be fruit, nuts or flowers. Sometimes a worshipper may give a small sum of money.

During worship it is the custom in some temples for people to place a dot or line of red powder on their foreheads. This is called a tilak or tikka and shows that they have been to worship. Its shape shows which god they worshipped. The tilak is rarely used in Britain with its religious significance, but it is often applied as 'make-up' or a fashion accessory. It should not be confused with the red dot many Indian women wear on their foreheads. This often just shows that they are married.

Hindus will be delighted if you want to visit a temple. You should learn as much about Hinduism as you can beforehand. Then contact the priest or a member of the committee, and ask permission to visit – this is particularly important if you want to take a group. Dress modestly and take off your shoes before going into the room containing the images. Remember the temple is a sacred place for Hindus and behave respectfully. Ask permission if you want to take photographs or make tape recordings. After your visit a thank you letter would be appreciated. From the Christian perspective don't go when worship is taking place and do have prayer support. Before entering, ask the Lord to protect you from any spiritual forces that may be present in a place where images are worshipped. It may be better to see a temple on video. There are useful video tapes available from many of the sources listed at the back of the book.

In India there are usually separate temples for different gods but this is not possible in Britain. Here you will often find a variety of images round the walls. They each represent a different god. Ghee lamps and incense sticks will usually be burning before them. There may be three or four small metal bowls round the room to contain prasad for the worshippers. There will also be a box for offerings. Individual devotees will come and worship the image of the particular god they venerate. Temples are also used for the celebration of festivals, religious discussions, recitals of Indian music and other activities. They are usually supported by the local Hindu business community who provide most of the financial backing.

Pilgrimages

Hindus are not obliged to go on pilgrimages but many do. In India during certain festivals they may make a short one to the temple of a god not far from their home. But many go on pilgrimages of over a thousand miles to well-known cities and temples. Those in Britain may return to India to make a pilgrimage for a special reason such as depositing in a holy river the ashes of a relative cremated in this country.

Some travel companies in Britain specialise in arranging group travel to Indian holy places. In India, people may make their own way on public transport but some think they gain more merit if they walk. This may be for hundreds of miles and take weeks or even months. When they arrive at a sacred place some pilgrims crawl round it on their hands and knees to show they are sorry for wrong things they have done.

Ascetic practices

As a sign of devotion to the gods, Hindus will often
submit to severe ascetic practices. In the West, the
common impression is that this involves people
sitting or lying on beds of nails, but this sort of
thing goes on less nowadays. However, in India,
some people may still climb long flights of steps
on their knees, or take a vow to keep silent for a
number of years, or sit or stand in one position for
days on end. Through these practices they hope
to gain enough merit to move to a higher level
in their next reincarnation. These practices are
not so noticeable in Britain because the business
community predominates and they do not usually
observe them.

Devout Hindus also fast regularly to receive
extra blessings or as a protection against evil.
This is a regular custom in Britain, especially
among the women.

Meditation

Most Hindus believe that meditation will help
to purify their mind and draw them closer to
Brahman. They may use a rosary of beads to help
them concentrate; or repeat the name of a god over
and over again up to many thousands of times.
This mantra, or name of god, always includes the
word Om, the most sacred of all sounds. (p. 60).
Hindu meditation consists of emptying the mind,
whereas Christian meditation involves filling it
with thoughts of God and is usually based on
Scripture.

Ritual purity

This is a central concept of Hinduism. Causes of pollution are numerous and include eating prohibited food, being in contact with human or animal emissions, breaking caste rules, touching an impure person or taking food from him. A family is polluted when a member dies or gives birth. A Hindu who is unclean should not touch religious objects, such as garlands of flowers used in worship, as he makes them impure. There are a great variety of methods of purification. The most usual is to have a bath under running water. It is particularly important to purify oneself in this way before worship.

However in Britain these restrictions are not always observed. 'A dilution of the religious experience is the price they are prepared to pay in order to enjoy a comfortable life style.'[3]

One devout Hindu left Britain and returned to India because he found it too difficult in this country to carry out all the devotional activities to which he had been accustomed.

Things to do

1. Ask a Hindu friend to tell you how he worships God. Then describe your own practice to him. Try not to get into an argument! Just use the conversation for exchanging information.

2. Ask a Hindu who grew up in India to tell you if there are any differences between the way he worshipped in India and the way he does so

in Britain. Ask if these differences have any significance or if they are just another way of doing things.

3. Visit a Hindu temple if you can, using the guidelines given in this chapter.

4. Get together with some other Christians and set up your own market stall. Sell cheaply-priced trinkets together with Christian books and booklets. But remember that the prime objective is to build up contacts.

SIX

HINDU FESTIVALS

Hindus base their calendar on the moon. Most festivals happen in the middle of the month when the moon is full or when the new moon is just about to appear. Some are only celebrated in certain regions of India, others all over the country. Some involve fasting and private worship in the home, others are celebrated publicly with the whole community taking part. Some are celebrated everywhere but the stories told about their origin vary from area to area. So do not be surprised if Hindu friends from different backgrounds tell you different things about a festival. Not all the festivals described in this chapter will happen in your area of Britain. You can ask Hindu friends which they observe.

Hindus in Britain do not feel able to observe festivals in the way they did in India. For example, in India, Diwali lasts for five days and these are public holidays for schools and colleges. Even office workers have two days off. But in Britain public holidays do not coincide with Diwali so Hindus have to limit their celebrations. Other festivals are celebrated on the nearest weekend to the actual dates on which they occur in India. Hindus also feel unable to celebrate as fully as

in India where most festivals take place out of
doors.

Navaratri

This festival takes place in September or October.
Navaratri means nine nights and this is how long
the festival lasts. It is celebrated by Hindus from
the state of Gujarat (Goojarat) in India. They
worship the goddess Parvati, the wife of Shiva. In
the home they place a small brass image of her on a
bed of rice in a copper dish and perform puja before
it twice a day. They also keep a lamp burning; and
each day they hang a garland of seasonal flowers
from a peg above the image. Members of the family
offer special food to the goddess at various times.
In Britain if the women of the household go out
to work it is often not possible to make a fresh
garland of flowers each day nor keep the lamp
burning continuously.

In this country during Navaratri some Hindu
families get together each night in a local hall
to enjoy singing devotional songs in praise of
the goddess and dancing stick dances, known
as raas garba. These are folk dances in which
people knock short sticks together to keep time.
They dance round a special shrine to Parvati. This
is a six-sided box with a cone-shaped top. On the
top is a lamp, and on each side of the box there is
a picture of a different goddess. The whole thing is
decorated with coloured lights and tinsel. During
the evening a priest performs the arati ceremony.
Lots of brass lamps are placed around the shrine

and people make offerings of fruit and sweets.
These are later given out as prasad.

In large cities in Britain the dances are often
organised by a small group of people who hire
a hall and musicians and then sell tickets for
the event, known as a garba night. Christians
are welcome to attend. Hindus dress extremely
smartly on such an occasion so Christians should
do so too – unless they wish to stand out like a
sore thumb.

In Bengal, on the eighth day of Navaratri,
Parvati is worshipped under one of her other
names, Durga. A large clay image of her, with
eight arms holding different weapons and riding a
tiger, is installed on a raised platform. In the story
of Rama he prayed to Durga when his wife was
captured. Hindus remember this at Navaratri,
offer puja to the image and dance round the
platform. At the end of the festival the image is
taken in procession through the town and thrown
into a river. Devotees believe it takes all their bad
luck with it.

Durga is also the symbol of mothers. Girls who
have been married in the past year try to return
home to visit their mothers for this festival if
they can.

Dusserah (Dussayra)

This festival is sometimes included as part of
Navaratri because it occurs on the day after. It
celebrates events from two great Hindu poems, the
Mahabharata and the *Ramayana* (p.82 and p.85)

In North India people celebrate Rama's defeat

of Ravana, king of Lanka. Rama was the eldest
son of the king of Ayodhya. (Ayodhya is the
place where Hindus recently destroyed a Muslim
mosque. They claimed it occupied the site of a
former Hindu temple, built over the spot where
Rama is said to have been born. The trouble there
sparked off disturbances all over India and also in
Britain.)

Rama entered an archery contest in a neigh-
bouring kingdom. As a reward for winning it he
was given the hand of Sita in marriage. The king of
Ayodhya had three queens. When Rama returned
home, the youngest demanded that her son be
made the heir to the throne and Rama be banished
from the kingdom for fourteen years. This queen
had once helped the king to win a battle and he
had made her certain promises which she now
demanded he fulfil. So Rama had to go and live in
the forest with Sita and his brother Lakshman.

One day Rama and Lakshman were away from
their dwelling place trying to catch a spotted deer
to which Sita had taken a fancy. While they were
doing so Ravana, the evil king of the island of
Lanka, kidnapped her.

Rama and Lakshman searched for her for many
days. In their wanderings they came to a southern
kingdom whose ruler, Sugriva, had been deposed
by his brother. Rama promised to help him regain
his throne and in return Sugriva sent his monkey
general, Hanuman, to look for Sita. Hanuman
finally discovered her being held a prisoner on
Lanka.

His monkey soldiers formed a bridge from the
mainland to the island and Rama, Sugriva and
their army crossed over to Lanka. In the battle

that followed Rama killed Ravana and rescued Sita.

Rama, Sita and Lakshman then returned to their father's kingdom. There were great celebrations and Rama was crowned king.

Dusserah celebrates the defeat of Ravana. Large figures of him and his helpers, made from bamboo and paper, are blown up with the fireworks.

Diwali

This is the most important Hindu festival and is celebrated all over India at the end of October or the beginning of November. For many Hindus it includes the New Year. In most places it lasts for five days but in some only three. Diwali means 'row of lights', so in Britain Hindus decorate the fronts of their houses with candles or a string of electric lights. They usually hire a hall for the festivities, which include fireworks for the children and a lavish meal for everyone. They also dance and sing to show their joy. Many Hindu clubs and temples arrange this dinner on the Saturday evening nearest to the actual days of Diwali.

Like many other festivals Diwali celebrates several stories. One of the most popular tells the story of how Rama rescued Sita and brought her home to Ayodhya, where he was crowned king. Other stories tell how the god Vishnu won a battle with the wicked giant, Narakasura, and how he tricked a king named Bali who was trying to take over the world. People in different parts of India think some of the stories more important than others,

so the festival is not celebrated in the same way
everywhere.

At Diwali, Hindus also remember Lakshmi, the
goddess of wealth. She is supposed to visit houses
that are clean and tidy and lit with lamps, and
brings good luck for the coming year. Lakshmi's
visit is very important to those who own shops
or businesses. Money, gold ornaments, cheque
books and account books, representing her, are
offered as puja. Businessmen make sure all their
debts are paid and make up their account books.
Hindu businessmen present theirs to Lakshmi in
the temple at a ceremony called chopra puja. The
next day they start new ones.

Diwali is a family festival. People give each
other presents and share meals. Sending cards is
becoming more popular, especially in Britain. The
idea of the festival is to show that just as darkness
can be driven away by light, so evil can be driven
away by good.

Hindus often say, 'Diwali is the same as your
Christmas', because of the feasting and the exchange of cards and presents. This comparison
is misleading. The origins of the two are totally
different, though the ways of celebrating them
may be superficially similar.

Mahashiva-Ratri

Mahashiva-Ratri which means 'Great Night of
Shiva', takes place in February or March. Shiva
is one of the most important gods in Hinduism.
He is believed to have the power to create and
destroy. Sometimes he is pictured dancing in a

circle of flames. One story says that the energy of Shiva's dance created the world, keeps it in existence and will destroy it one day. Then he will start to dance again and the cycle of creation will begin once more. He will repeat this numerous times.

In some stories Shiva is said to perform this dance on Mahashiva-Ratri. It is really neither a festival nor a feast but a fast. The devotees of Shiva go without food for twenty-four hours and offer worship to his image between midnight and sunrise. They do so by repeating his name and placing flowers and fruit in front of the image. Then they pour water in a steady stream from a container suspended above it. At sunrise the worshipper goes home, bathes and breaks the fast.

Holi

Holi takes place in the spring, either late February or early March. In India the whole festival lasts five days. People light bonfires and fireworks, burn figures of demons, and dance. In Britain they may light a bonfire on an open space near a temple or public hall hired for the occasion. They tell stories about the god Krishna, especially of his youth when he is said to have played many tricks on people. So Hindus play practical jokes on each other at Holi. In India, on the last day, people throw coloured water over friends and strangers in the streets – they wear their oldest clothes to avoid spoiling good ones. To go home covered in colours is a sign that you have had a good time. Some Hindu parents in Britain allow their children to

have fun throwing coloured water over each other
in their own gardens but otherwise this part of
the festival is not practised in this country. One
elderly Hindu living in Britain said, 'It's not the
same here. People have become too sophisticated
to play at Holi as we did in India.'

Rama Navami

This festival celebrates the birthday of the god
Rama and is especially popular with Hindus from
North India. It takes place in April. The celebrations, which include stories from the *Ramayana*
(p. 85), happen at home but people also go to the
temple if they can. As a special part of the worship
they sing the *Ramanama*, a list of all the names of
Rama.

Rama Navami is a fast day when Hindus do not
eat certain foods, including rice and vegetables.
Other foods, which most of them could not normally afford, are eaten instead.

On the day of the full moon, in the same month,
the birth of Hanuman the monkey god, is also
celebrated.

Raksha Bandhan

This festival is sometimes called brother-sister
day. It takes place in August. Raksha means
'protection' and Bandhan means 'to tie'. This
festival reminds people of a story about the god
Indra. An evil monster attacked him, but his wife
saved him by tying a magic string round his wrist.

Hindu girls tie red and gold bracelets, made of thread or tinsel, round their brothers' wrists. This thread is called a raksha or rakhi. By her action the girl shows that she has chosen her brother as her protector. She also uses the occasion to give her blessing to him and assure him of her protection too. In return he usually gives her a present. Friends also exchange threads as a sign of renewed friendship.

Janami-Ashtami

This also takes place in August and celebrates the birthday of the god Krishna. He is supposed to have been born at midnight so many Hindus spend all night in the temple. In India they celebrate by blowing conch shells and saying loud prayers at the time of his birth. They sing, dance and share special sweets. One Hindu in Britain observed, 'If we did that here we'd have trouble from the people around because you know we pray *loudly*.'

The following day is a fast day. No one eats till evening when they enjoy a feast to celebrate the birth. Many temples contain an image or picture of the baby Krishna. This is put into a swing or cot decorated with flowers. People take turns to push this to 'amuse the "baby".' They also perform plays and songs about Krishna.

Things to do

1. Ask a Hindu friend to tell you which festivals she celebrates and why.

2. Find out from her the dates of the local Hindu festivals. Ask if you may visit her family then. Most Hindus will be delighted that you want to do this.

3. A few days before the festival ask her to tell you the story behind it and to explain what the worshippers do.

4. After you have attended the Hindu festival invite your friend to come to church with you at Christmas or Easter. Don't just expect her to turn up – arrange a meeting place on the way or call for her. A few days beforehand tell her the story of what is being celebrated and explain what will happen in the service. This will help her to feel less strange.

5. Hindus love music. If you know some young Asian Christians, get together with them, to hold an evening of Bhangra dancing. You could perhaps do this for Diwali. Above all, pray about doing something practical. Then act on what the Lord tells you, as soon as possible.

6. South Asian Concern organises an alternative Christian Diwali. You can write to them for details at the address given in the Useful Addresses section.

SEVEN

THE HINDU SCRIPTURES

J ust as for Christians the Bible is the prime
source book to guide us through our lives, so
Hindus have scriptures of their own, to serve a
similar purpose. But the Hindu concept of time
and history is different from that of the Bible. The
Bible is rooted in actual events but much of the
Hindu scriptures are unashamedly mythological.
There is no historical evidence for many of the
events described. For Vijay, finding that the Bible
was a historic document rooted in history was a
breath of fresh air in his spiritual searching and
striving. It was a key aspect of his conversion from
Hinduism.

The Hindu scriptures are like one more idol,
though the most precious. They must be treated
reverently and with extreme respect. They have
pride of place in temples, being placed on special
lecterns of their own. Hindus see the Bible as a
similar talisman, so don't underline verses, turn
down corners, physically mistreat it, carry it about
in your coat pocket, put it on the floor or even in a
bag on the floor if they are going to see it.

Because Hinduism has developed over thousands of years, there are hundreds of Hindu
holy books. Some are not read often but others

are still extremely important. Most of them are in
Sanskrit. Hindus do not know much about their
own scriptures, even though they reverence them
so highly, and few will know all that is covered in
this chapter.

The *Vedas*

These are the oldest holy books and go back in
written form to about 1200 BC. For about 2,000
years before that they were handed down by word
of mouth.

The first one, the *Rig Veda*, is the most important. It includes over a thousand hymns and
poems praising various gods and is divided into
ten books. Varuna, the creative force, and Indra,
the storm god, are the best known deities of these
times. Today Hindus still worship some of the
Vedic gods, especially the god of fire, worshipped
in the havan (p. 63). Many Hindus recite the
Gayatri or Sun hymn daily. Rudra, a minor Vedic
deity, developed into Shiva, the destroyer and
creator. Vishnu was a minor god in the *Vedas*.

The *Rig Veda*, sometimes written in English as
the *Rg Veda*, contains an account of the creation
myth. But it is much more vague than the Genesis
account. Here are some verses from it:

Who knows for sure, who can declare,
Whence sprang creation, created where?
The gods came later, they were not aware
To answer this riddle, who else can dare?

From birth pangs of toiling sea,

The majestic year came to be,
Lord of the processional night and day
Who holds life's cycle in his imperial sway.

The creator made the sky and earth.
Sun and moon he gave their birth,
The celestial world he put in place
And in between, the boundless space.

The other *Vedas* contain instructions to the priests about worship and descriptions of religious ceremonies.

The vedic rituals are rarely practised and most of the hymns are little known. But they can still be enjoyed as poetry or speculative thinking on the causes of the universe. At their heart, they acknowledge the sinfulness of humanity, deserving a death which can only be avoided by sacrifice. Originally grain and animal sacrifices were performed. Around 700 BC the *Upanishads* began to interpret this tradition to mean that a life filled with selfless activity is the correct way to use god-given abilities. One must act without desire for reward.

The *Upanishads*

The word *Upanishad* means 'sit down near' which is how the teachings began. People who wanted to learn from wise men would sit around them and receive instruction. The *Upanishads* contain philosophical teachings about the most common Hindu beliefs, including all those mentioned in

Chapter Three. They are particularly difficult
to understand, requiring a teacher, or guru to
explain their meaning. They were the inspiration
for later philosophy too.

Among them are dialogues in which the situations and characters help to illustrate the teaching. For example Yajnavalkya's long dialogue
with King Janaka in one of the *Upanishads*
or his shorter one with his wife, help us to
understand that Brahman is pure consciousness
without an object. Another contrasts learning with
wisdom and contains a series of illustrations about
Brahman.

These *Upanishads* speak of Brahman mainly
as an impersonal being. But others, such as the
shorter *Isha Upanishad*, speak of a personal god.
Another suggests that salvation comes to those
whom God chooses. The first half of the *Katha
Upanishad* tells the story of a wise brahmin boy's
confrontation with death; its analysis of personality, which it likens to a chariot, is a fruitful basis
for discussion.

Mahabharata (Ma-ha-bharat-a)

This epic is said to contain 100,000 verses in
eighteen books, though there are various editions
of different lengths and emphases. It is the longest
poem in the world and was written by many people
over several hundreds of years. Scholars believe
the *Mahabharata* reached its present form about
AD 300 but it did not become popular until the
ninth century AD. Many stories with a moral
message are woven round the central narrative:

What it really is is an encyclopedia of dharma, righteous behaviour. Do you want to know how an officer should teach his soldiers or a grandfather advise his grandsons? Should a man who has been wronged seek vengeance or turn the other cheek? What can a mother do when she finds her children have grown up reckless and evil minded? Answers to these and innumerable other questions are found in this astonishing book, through myths and legends, dialogues and scraps of history.[1]

The most important story tells of two royal families who were cousins. They fought over which of them should rule the kingdom. One family tricked the other several times, until at last they fought a great battle, after which the rightful heir gained the throne.

It is important to understand that the *Mahabharata* is not a historical book though it may appear to be at first glance. It is a Hindu story, part of which, the *Bhagavad-Gita*, is the best loved Hindu text of all.

The *Bhagavad-Gita* (Bhag-vad-geeta)

The *Bhagavad-Gita* (the Song of the Lord) occurs in the sixth book of the *Mahabharata* and contains 700 verses divided into eighteen chapters. Hindus usually refer to it as the *Gita*. They read it more than any other scripture.

On the evening before the great battle (see above) Arjuna, one of the brothers, is filled with remorse at the thought of killing his own relatives to gain the kingdom. He talks about his feelings to his charioteer who turns out to be the god Krishna in disguise. The dialogue between them forms the substance of the *Gita*.

Krishna instructs Arjuna in moral and religious values and man's relations to God. His main themes are:

a. Everyone has a moral duty to work without expecting any return and to uphold the teaching about dharma (duty).

b. A devotee should express his devotion to a personal god in worship – the way of bhakti.

c. The soul (atman) is indestructible and after death is reborn into a new body determined by its actions in its previous life. One should not grieve over death but continue to perform one's moral duty to the best of one's ability.

d. The supreme spirit Brahman is eternal and everything in the universe is part of it.

e. There are no pre-determined moral standards as there are in the Bible; our motive for doing something determines whether it is right or wrong. Krishna also describes all the yogas and how to practise them.

John Bowker says, 'Close to the heart of almost every Hindu is the *Gita*.'[2] He goes on to quote what some Hindus say about it:

The *Gita* contains the answer to all problems – or at least all the problems that

really matter – though it is recognised as
being difficult to understand in depth. It
may require a guide; and the reliable guide
can only be picked out or discerned by his
or her own behaviour, not by some external
qualification.[3]

If you read the *Gita* and if you can
understand it, you'll find the answer to
all your questions. The only question is,
whether you can understand what is
written there.
    But if you can't understand it, to whom
do you go for guidance?
    In this country, I think, the question is
difficult: it's very difficult to find an expert
person. But when somebody comes from
India or somewhere else and has authority,
and has achieved or reached that level, we
used to ask him.[4]

The *Ramayana* (Ram-ay-ana)

This is another long poem, though much shorter
than the *Mahabharata*. It contains 24,000 verses
in seven books. The incidents in it are said to
have taken place before those of the *Mahabharata*
though it was written down later. It tells the story
of the god Rama and his wife Sita (pp. 72–73).
    A great many Hindus worship Rama. He is
honoured as the model of an obedient son, virtu-
ous husband, dutiful king, loving brother, brave
warrior and generous conqueror. He put his duty
before his personal happiness. Other characters

are represented as ideals of Hindu virtues – Sita, the constant wife, Lakshman, the affectionate brother, Hanuman, the loyal servant. Taken as a whole the story shows the perpetual struggle between good and evil forces in the world.

Puranas

The *Puranas* were composed between the sixth and sixteenth centuries AD and are used mainly by temple priests. There are many minor *Puranas* but traditionally there are eighteen important ones. They deal mainly with the worship of Brahma, the creator, Vishnu, the sustainer, and Shiva, the destroyer.

The most widely read is the *Bhagavata* (*Bhagavata*) *Purana*. The legends praise Vishnu and his incarnations (avatars) especially Krishna. The tenth book gives a detailed biography of Krishna and is the most frequently read. There are many translations of, and commentaries on, this text.

The Laws of Manu

These are obscure texts not read by the ordinary Hindu. If you do want to read about them consult David Burnett's book, *The Spirit of Hinduism*.

Hindu scriptures differ from one another in style in the same way as say, in the Bible, the historical and the law books, the Wisdom literature and the Epistles differ from each other. The *Rig Veda* could be seen as vaguely parallel to the Psalms. It was written at about the same time.

Hindu texts are often scarce on teaching about how to relate to normal human beings or everyday life. You can learn how a king should relate to his courtiers but not how to relate to the person next door. Some texts are very unclear, and many Hindus read them out of a sense of duty rather than because they understand them. Most of them are long and wordy and very few Hindus are directly familiar with all of them. They have neither the time nor the inclination to read them. As they are not 'user-friendly' books, they need professional priests and gurus to teach what they say. There has been no real reformation in Hinduism which might have delivered the faith back into the hands of the common people. The average Hindu family relies heavily on priests and gurus as religious authority figures.

The original texts are in Sanskrit. English translations are not valid for prayer, because the sounds of the words are important. Second generation British Hindus are usually totally unfamiliar with Sanskrit and other Asian languages. The texts are rare and expensive to purchase. Only one version of each text is authorised for publication, not dozens of different translations as with the Bible. Commentaries are few and devotional books non-existent. At the popular level, comic books of the *Mahabharata* are available but there is no middle ground theological teaching. 'Correctly handling the word of truth' (2 Timothy 2:15) does not figure in Hindu thought.

The issue for Hindus is not whether they understand scripture. The core of the matter is that it is a ritual object, as is the Bible for some nominal Christians. You cannot derive Hindu theology

from Hindu scripture in the way that you can
Christian theology from the Bible. Attempting to
do so has led many well-meaning Christians up
a blind alley. One strand of Hindu scripture will
lead you to the conclusion that Hinduism teaches
you that reality is all one, while another will lead
you to the conclusion that God is in everything.
All is relative and nothing is absolute. Much is
contradictory. Few Hindus bother to really try and
understand them. They have no more impact on
the daily life of the average Hindu than the Bible
has on the life of a non-Christian. Those who do
read and understand are often troubled by what
they read. In *Death of a Guru* the author tells us
about one Hindu whose reading of scripture nearly
led him to kill his aunt. Some would conclude that
the pudding has been spiked with something very
unpleasant.

However some Hindus do read their scriptures,
at least the *Gita*, regularly. But we should not
assume that they all do. Some dislike the idea of
ordering their lives by written instructions, even
those in holy books. Others read only as the mood
takes them:

Mr. Krishan Mital, President of the Hindu
Cultural Society in Bradford says, 'I'm not
one, I should say, to perform any definite
worship. But I do say some shlokas and
mantras from the scriptures whenever I
feel like it. It depends on my mood – on
my temper, I should say. Sometimes you
are under strain and then you remember
straight away. Sometimes you are thinking
about some of your personal problems,

say financial problems, say you had a
slight row with your wife, or in the family,
and you are a bit upset; then you think.
And when you contemplate in that way,
straightaway you realise and go back to
your religious teachings of the scriptures,
and then suddenly something comes up,
and it resolves this problem.[5]

Hindu teachers from India visit Britain regularly.
They set up large tents in areas where there
are many Hindus and read the *Ramayama* or
Mahabharata. These meetings sometimes go on
for weeks and attract thousands of Hindus. Many
Hindu families buy video and audio tapes of these
meetings and use them regularly in their homes.

Things to do

1. Ask a Hindu friend if he reads a holy book regularly. If he does ask him why it is important to
   him. But don't be surprised if he doesn't know
   much about any of the Hindu scriptures.

2. Ask him to tell you the story of the scripture
   he reads and the teaching he finds in it.

3. Try to discover if he puts what he reads into
   practice, or just reads the scripture as a duty
   or to gain merit.

4. The Hindu scriptures themselves are hard for a
   Westerner to understand. However there are a
   number of books about them written for school

children in Britain which you would find helpful. Try to get hold of one (see the book list at
the back of this book) and study it.

5. You should however try to read the *Bhagavad
Gita* (several editions are available in English).
It will only take you a couple of hours and
it will give you first hand knowledge of the
most widely used Hindu text. The translation
by Easwaran, published by Arkana is particularly readable. It has a helpful introduction and
notes.

EIGHT

HINDU SECTS AND PHILOSOPHIES

Hinduism can embrace almost every religious teaching and practice that exists. The one common factor is the claim that there is no absolute truth. Therefore Hindus are totally opposed to the Christian claim that Jesus is the only way to God. The practice of Hinduism varies and an individual has complete freedom of choice of a personal god, method of worship, and performance of rituals. This has given endless scope to those who want to develop their own splinter groups. Seekers who want to receive guidance for their lives have gathered round them. Most of the groups represented in Britain today are of fairly recent origin. Some like the Arya Samaj, Ramakrishna Mission, and Swami Narayan movement date from the latter half of the nineteenth century. Others have only developed since the Second World War.

Like the cults and sects which have sprung up around Christianity, most Hindu sects revolve around an authority figure – a religious leader, teacher and guru. Vishal Mangalwadi, in his book *World of the Gurus*, has unpacked some of the motives which cause Hindus and Westerners alike to follow these popular religious leaders.

Vishal attributes the rise of guruism to: a response to the traditional authority structures of the Indian family; a reaction to the extreme narrow-mindedness of Hindu society; a decrease in traditional religious authority; a reaction to empty materialism; and a disappointment with barren philosophy. Such a mishmash of fear, anxiety and mental anguish breaks down a person's security. It leaves him like a blank slate upon which a guru, like a father-figure, can write whatever he likes and have it accepted by a follower who is desperate for something in which to believe.

Vishal writes:

You cannot ask whether a guru's theories
are true. You just 'believe' and 'by faith'
accept them. 'But faith in what?' you may
enquire. Well, faith in the guru himself. He
is in touch with the infinite. He can serve
lepers or feed his elephants chocolate or
have sex with his male and female
followers. But he cannot be judged – he
is God! Infallible! Inscrutable! You simply
bow before him! Thou shalt not think, but
believe what the guru says![1]

Man needs to have religious teachers and spiritual movements because of his need for a satisfying view of life. This enables him to live through its struggles. The following gurus and movements attempt to offer a guide-book or map to make sense of life and to live it meaningfully.

The question which their followers need to ask is, 'Can this be true?' But when they accept the view that 'truth is relative' they have thrown away any chance of having a firm foundation from which to judge their own experiences and the teaching of their spiritual leaders. They can only be rescued by discovering real truth through meeting Christ, who is the physical expression of truth.

The Arya Samaj

The Arya Samaj (Society of Aryans) was formed in 1875. It maintains that the Vedas are a complete revelation of God. It accepts the doctrines of karma and reincarnation but holds that the soul cannot be lost in the supreme spirit. It opposes image worship, animal sacrifice, many of the main Hindu festivals, caste, untouchability, pilgrimages, ritual bathing and the segregation of women.

In Britain they meet together on Sundays to worship the sacred fire, chanting passages from the Vedas and reciting the Gayatri hymn (p. 80) After worship everyone shares cooked food. This is to help break down traditional caste barriers and affirm that all members are equal.

The Arya Samaj is missionary minded and is especially concerned to win back Hindus who have converted to Christianity or Islam. It emphasises education and social reform and expects followers to help others in need. Members have to give a regular percentage of their income to the Society's funds. Every member has to practise austerity and self-discipline. They should eat and drink only what is necessary to sustain life, forego any form of extravagance and have only the possessions needed for a simple life-style.

The Ramakrishna Mission

The best known leader of this group was Swami
Vivekananda (1863-1902), a disciple of Sri Rama
Krishna. He travelled in both India and the West,
declaring that although all religions were true,
Hinduism was the mother of them all.

He held that every soul was potentially divine
and that a person should aim to achieve inner
divinity by learning to exercise control of his body,
mind and spirit. He did not believe that rituals
and temple worship were important. Vivekananda
also declared that service to mankind was the
best religion in the world. He tried to re-interpret
the Vedantic system so as to accommodate the
biblical idea of selfless service to people because
they are human beings. During his travels he
founded Ramakrishna missions all over the world
which promote educational, social and spiritual
activities. The missions run schools, orphanages
and hospitals in pursuit of their goal of serving
mankind.

Swami Narayana

This sect was founded by Sahajananda Swami in
1824 in the western Indian state of Gujarat. His
followers believed him to be an incarnation of
Vishnu and gave him the name Swami Narayana.

They accept the authority of the Vedas but hope
to achieve moksha through worshipping their
founder. They emphasise moral duty (dharma)
as well as earning money and enjoying the good
things of life. They practise congregational worship of several gods. They believe in karma and

reincarnation and celebrate the important Hindu
festivals and life-cycle rituals. But they reject caste.
Many self-governing Swami Narayana branches
exist in India and Britain. In this country Gujarati
businessmen support the Swami Narayana movement. Most of them came to this country from
East Africa. They are prosperous and do a great
deal of charitable work. There are 35,000-40,000
Swami Narayana followers in Great Britain who
are hardworking and law abiding.

The Radha Soami Satsang

This sect has its headquarters at Beas in the Indian
Punjab. Successive leaders have been known as
'The Master'. Prospective devotees individually
have a special session with 'The Master' when
he gives them the 'Name' of God. The 'Name' is
the term for the five mantras on which they must
meditate for two and a half hours daily. They do
this by concentrating on the 'third eye' together
with the recitation of the 'Name'. The third eye
is supposed to be in the forehead, above the nose
and between the eyebrows. It is the eye of the
spirit. As they recite the 'Name' the third eye is
believed to open. The devotees then gradually lose
body consciousness. They begin to see visions and
hear the 'Word'. The 'Word' is said to be the divine
sound current within. Radha Soamis believe this
permeates the entire universe and then goes back
to God. When the soul contacts the 'word' it merges
into it and begins to travel towards God with it. All
Radha Soamis must be vegetarian and teetotal.
    The Radha Soami Satsang draws its beliefs from

Hindu, Muslim, Sikh and Christian sources and
seeks to encompass them all in its own system.
However in doing so it has become confused at
many points. It maintains that God is without
personality and without a name. Despite this it
still attributes to him qualities of love, grace,
wisdom and power. It also believes in a negative
power, the Universal Mind, the devil, and says
that most people mistake him for the supreme
God. Radha Soamis frequently quote the Bible to
prove their beliefs but almost always completely
out of context.

In Britain Radha Soami followers meet each
weekend to attend a satsang (religious gather-
ing). Here they sing devotional hymns and hear
taped messages from the Master. They place great
emphasis on theoretical teaching and religious
discussion and have published many books.

The Radha Soami Satsang has a wide following
in Europe and North America. There are more
Western than Indian members of this sect.

The Hare Krishna Movement

This movement originated in India in the sixteenth century but did not reach the West till
the 1960s. Devotees worship Krishna and proclaim the prayer chant, the Hare Krishna mantra,
publicly. This has given them the name the Hare
Krishna Movement though its correct title is the
International Society for Krishna Consciousness
(ISKCON). 'Hare' means 'Lord' and 'Krishna' is
the name of the god they worship. When the movement first spread to the West in the 60s and 70s,

one saw shaven-headed, saffron-robed youngsters
on the streets of Britain distributing literature
and asking for a donation. Most of them have
now abandoned their distinctive appearance and
dress like anyone else. But they regularly march,
chanting, round the Leicester Square/Piccadilly
area of London. They also operate a vegetarian
restaurant in Soho.

The first temple in Britain opened in 1969. As
well as attracting young Westerners, it also drew
in young Hindus of Asian background because of
the elaborate puja performed in the temple. They
had only ever seen the simple worship of their
parents' household gods. One of the largest and
most popular temples in England is the Hare
Krishna Centre near Watford.

The group worship Krishna as the supreme
incarnation of the Lord, the absolute truth. To
truly show his loving devotion to Krishna a follower must give up the ties of his family and job.
He must not eat meat nor use drugs or alcohol.

In the 80s, the group appeal lessened, as far as
most young people were concerned, but now many
wealthy Indians are associating with the group as
British people might belong to the Rotary club or
the Freemasons.

There are superficial similarities to Christianity.
Devotion to a personal God and salvation through
him is a marked feature of both faiths. Hare
Krishna followers trying to convert Westerners
will major on this.

However the differences are actually immense.
Hare Krishnas believe in many gods, Krishna
being the chief one. They worship images of him,
teach that Jesus was a devotee of Krishna and

claim the Bible has been misinterpreted. Some of
the stories about Krishna seem to Christians to
depict him as immoral though Hindus and Hare
Krishnas see his actions as just youthful pranks.
By contrast Jesus is holy and without sin.

Hare Krishnas do not believe actions are intrin-
sically good or bad. They depend on the teachings
of one or other of their gurus and these teachings
vary. Jesus set standards which are the same for
every person and every situation for all time.

The Sathya Sai Baba Movement

The guru Sathya Sai Baba was born in India
in 1926. From the age of fourteen he began to
perform miracles and attract followers. In India
he has millions of devotees.

Sathya Sai Baba makes extravagant claims for
himself. In 1962 he claimed to be greater than
Rama and Krishna. In 1963 he declared himself an incarnation of Shiva. Since Westerners
began to join the movement he has also said he
is Jesus come again to establish righteousness in
the world.

His popularity rests chiefly on his miracles,
though some of them have been exposed as frauds
and he has always refused to have their authen-
ticity investigated.

He teaches that what is wrong in one situation
can be right in another. And also that what is
wrong for one person may be right for a higher
being. Disillusioned devotees claim that Sathya
Sai Baba uses the statement as an excuse to live
an immoral life. Certainly he has employed the

money given by his followers to live in style, with expensive cars and business dealings running into millions of pounds.

The movement was brought to Britain by a small number of his followers in 1966. Since then it has grown. The devotees usually meet for the singing of devotional songs and offer worship to a photograph of the guru.

A good Christian reference book on Sai Baba is *Lord of The Air* by Tal Brooke (see the book list at the back of this book).

Transcendental Meditation (TM)

TM was introduced to the West by Maharishi Mahesh Yogi. The title 'Maharishi' means 'Great Seer'. In 1957 he began to teach TM in India. However he found Indians reluctant to accept his system so he came to the West in 1959.

He is better known here than any other Hindu guru because of the conversion of the Beatles to TM. They soon gave it up however, John Lennon describing it as 'just a waste of time'.

Much of the Maharishi's teaching is based on Hinduism. He advertises TM as being not a religion but 'a simple technique for realising your full mental potential and attaining a deep sense of rest'. However, a devotee is expected to do puja before a picture of Guru Dev, the Maharishi's original teacher, and recite Sanskrit prayers. The Maharishi also gives each of his followers a mantra on which to meditate for twenty minutes morning and evening. These mantras are closely linked with the names of Hindu gods. The Maharishi claims that during meditation an individual is relieved of tensions, attains peace, gets in tune with all the laws of the universe and therefore automatically does what is good and right.

He also teaches that the goal of meditation is to empty one's mind. But this opens it to the entry of evil forces (Matthew 12:43–45) and the possibility of demon possession. Some ex-TM meditators have testified to this.

Several court cases have proved that the Maharishi has lied in claiming that TM is not a religion. But lying is permissible in his system because he claims that ultimately nothing in it can be false.

It is not easy to witness to TM followers. They will resent criticism of the Maharishi. Many of them feel that TM is superior to Christianity, and have been warned not to confuse themselves by considering other views. If an individual has been badly affected by this meditating, his thinking may also be muddled. Try to find out what led him into TM and pray for opportunities to show him that his desires can be more than satisfied in a personal relationship with Jesus.

Bhagwan Shree Rajneesh

Bhagwan Shree Rajneesh was a guru who established a commune at Pune in India in 1967. His teaching attracted wealthy young people who had dropped out of Indian and Western society. His devotees call him the Enlightened One and say he was God personified – in fact his title 'Bhagwan' means 'God'.

He taught that personal satisfaction is not found through reason but through an emotional trip.

Some of his meditation involves violent physical activity, hard breathing and shaking of the body in order to attain a state of ecstasy which he called enlightenment. He said that sex is a special way of experiencing the ultimate oneness of the universe, so he encouraged free love – he changed this teaching when AIDS hit the news headlines.

He was familiar with the teaching of Hinduism, Buddhism and Christianity and freely quoted, misquoted and misinterpreted them. For instance, he interpreted Jesus' words 'you must be born again' to mean that you must have sexual meditation. In his view man is not a sinner; he suggested he is in a mess but was not clear what the problem is.

Like the Maharishi, he taught that emptying one's mind is the way to experience God. However as we said before, the Bible teaches that this leaves it open to the entry of demons (p. 100).

Rajneesh became a millionaire several times over. He had ninety Rolls-Royces and an armed security guard! In 1981 he left India to found a new colony in the USA. But when some of his followers contravened American immigration laws he fled the country in his private jet. After that he tried to settle in Great Britain, Eire and South America, but in 1991 he returned to India where he died the same year.

When witnessing to people from this group do not criticise Rajneesh or his teaching or try to reason them out of their beliefs; they are unlikely to respond to this approach. You could ask them about their life before joining the group and get them to tell you about their families and what matters most to them. Pray for opportunities to share your own faith and then compare Rajneesh's teaching with that of Jesus. If someone becomes interested in Christianity you will need much love and patience to help him sort out truth from error. He will also need help to stand against former Rajneesh followers who will try to draw him back.

The New Age

In the last thirty years many different strands of Hindu teaching have become popular in Britain. As people have achieved material prosperity many have become aware of an inner emptiness. Various sects claiming to fill this have grown up, some of which we have already discussed. The New Age teaching is the most attractice to a growing number of people. Some of them have turned to astrologers who say that for the last 2,000 years we have been in the age of the fish, a Christian sign. Now we are moving into a New Age, the age of Aquarius, the water carrier. Water represents the spirit and this New Age will see growing spiritual awareness and the development of spiritual gifts.

When you meet people who claim to experience these, be careful. Christians also experience the Holy Spirit working in their lives. Ask God to enable you to discern the false from the true. Is Christ recognized as Lord in the person's life? Is the glory being given to Him? What fruits of the Spirit are being demonstrated in that individual's life?

A number of New Age groups share the search for personal wholeness. They use differing methods for trying to achieve it, which does not trouble them as they believe different people realise their full potential in different ways. Each year they hold a festival of Body, Mind and Spirit in London. Here all the New Age groups come together to learn more about how to achieve wholeness.

A great deal of their teaching has its origins in Hindu philosophy and the teaching of the gurus. (The video *Gods of the New Age* gives further information about this.) But New Age followers are not predominantly of Asian origin. Its teaching leaves the sovereignty of God out of the picture. Sin and failure are not seen as problems but rather as man's defective understanding of himself and the world. Once this is changed he will be able to achieve personal goodness. Because they claim men and women find their full potential in many different ways they oppose Christ's claim that he is the only way to God. They also deny that a personal relationship with him is the only way to true peace. They see no significance in Jesus' death on the Cross nor do they have a sense of God as someone who must be obeyed.

Happily, many Hindus have found their way through the maze of Asian thought and into the arms of Christ. Take Sheela, for example.

Sheela's story

I was born in India but when I was eighteen I went to Kenya to be married. After five years my husband died and I was left with four small children. But, because we are an extended family, my brother-in-law cared for us.

In 1966 the whole family left Kenya and

came to Britain. We found it very difficult
coming to a strange country and adjusting
to the different lifestyle.

I was a practising Hindu but was finding
that Hinduism did not satisfy me. I started
searching for an answer to my difficulties.
One day I shouted out to God, 'Please come
and help me.'

Shortly afterwards a friend, who knew
I was seeking for an answer, suggested I
try the Radha Soamis. So I did. My whole
family went to their headquarters at Beas
in the Indian Punjab. I took an oath not
to eat meat or eggs. The Master gave me a
mantra on which to meditate. I repeated
it daily for two and a half hour but still
didn't have peace and security. Then I
began to think, 'I became a Radha Soami to
receive peace. If I haven't got it I have been
cheated.' I asked God, 'I do all the correct
things. Why haven't I got peace?'

By this time one of my sons was working
in Switzerland. I went to visit him and his
family. He told me he had become a Christian
and invited me to accompany him to church.
I said, 'No. I have no experience of church.'
But he kept a Bible on the table in the sitting
room. The next day I picked it up and started
to read it. At once it interested me. After two
weeks I wanted to go to church. I found it
very different from what I had imagined. The
people were so caring and friendly.

When I returned home I started to read
the Bible regularly, and also *Death of a
Guru* and *I Dared to Call Him Father*. Also a

Christian friend came to see me and talked
about Jesus. My son in Switzerland did too.
Very, very slowly I began to
understand. I had no sudden dramatic
experience.

Two years later I again went to
Switzerland. There I was baptised.

When I returned to Britain I was afraid
to tell my in-laws what I had done. But
my behaviour changed and they saw I was
different. Eventually I told them why. At
first they totally ignored me. Then they got
very angry. But time is a healer and finally
when they saw I was happy they accepted
what I had done.

It was a long time before I was able
to speak to Hindu friends about Jesus.
Now I can boldly tell them about my faith.
Sometimes they ask questions and I pray to
God for the right answer.

I now have peace and security. I pray and
get so many answers. I don't ask for money
and things like that. I pray that God will
use me. I read the Bible and pray before
breakfast.

God has worked so many miracles in my
life. For two and a half years I suffered
severe pain in my back and hips. But I have
recently had an operation and now I'm fine.
God gave me back my health and I can go
out and do things. Now I appreciate those
years. They brought me very close to God.
Sometimes I fought him and felt I hated
him. But in the end I said, 'You know best.'

One night in a dream I said, 'Lord, I want

you.' I felt a soft hand in mine and he said,
'I am always with you.' I opened my eyes
and said, 'Yes.' Everything was dark but I
felt safe with him.

I love the Bible, especially Hebrews 11,
Peter's letters and many of the Psalms. But
I find the Old Testament very difficult to
understand.

In Hinduism I never had the peace and
security I have now. In that religion there
are so many gods and so many images. I
never knew which was the true god.

Some of the Hindu gurus, like Sai Baba,
do miracles. He does things like conjuring
an apple or ashes out of his hand. But the
miracles of Jesus were so different. They
helped people. Jesus was humble and never
did things to show off. He is my Saviour and
I will always love him.

Things to do

1. Think through or discuss how you would show
   a Hindu that God is personal.

2. Work out how you would explain to a Hindu the
   Christian teaching on atoning for one's sins.

3. Obtain a video of the life of Jesus and invite
   Hindu friends to come and watch it. Serve
   some light refreshments at the end and use
   the opportunity to ask your friends what they
   thought of the film. (See lists of societies and
   organisations who can supply visual aids, at
   the back of the book.)

NINE
HINDUISM IN BRITAIN

Until the 1960s, only a small number of Indian intellectuals and gurus brought Hinduism to Britain. Some of them founded the Vedanta Society, which established the first public place of worship for Hindus in Muswell Hill, in north London, in 1949. But until the late 1950s only about 70,000 Indians resided permanently in Britain and not all of them were Hindus. Then came the flood of immigrants from South Asia, which included many Hindus. They were mostly less educated and brought with them the popular form of Hinduism.

But, as we have seen in earlier chapters, there is no standard form of Hindu worship, of celebrating festivals, or of performing rituals, even in India. To travel from north to south India takes four days by train. There are fifteen major languages and over 600 minor ones in the country.[1] The climate varies a great deal too, and these differences have given rise to a wide variety of customs. However in Britain Hindus do have some basic practices and experiences in common. They have changed their worship patterns and the way they celebrate festivals and conduct life-cycle rituals to suit local circumstances.

Hindu Temples in Britain

Throughout the 1960s Hindus usually met for worship in private homes. These gatherings started for the extended family but later expanded to include like-minded devotees from outside. During these years many Hindus pooled resources to form temple trusts. They hoped eventually to purchase a property and establish a temple. Hindus in Leicester were the first to achieve this goal in 1969. Shortly afterwards temples were established in various parts of London, and in Coventry, Bradford and Leeds. Then the number of Hindu temples grew rapidly. There are now over 100 in Britain. In some places Gujarati and Punjabi Hindus share the same temple and facilities. In others they have separate places of worship. Over the years many have imported marble images from India. Most temples now have several images, placed in prominent positions in the main hall.

Lay leadership

Very few Hindu priests came to Britain in the early days. Local lay people, usually of the brahmin caste, supervised the worship and performed the Hindu rites. Even in marriages, members of the families played the part of the priest. Most people did not like this but as there was no alternative they had to accept it. However as time went on, more priests gained entry to Britain and lay people ceased to conduct daily worship or carry out the traditional ceremonies.

Nevertheless lay people in Britain are taking a much more vocal part in speaking about their religion than they would in India. There, only brahmins or gurus speak in public about Hindu beliefs and customs, but in British society we expect representatives of different ethnic backgrounds to speak on behalf of their community. So though the priest may do so, in this country it is more often lay people who speak out about Hinduism.

Hindu Associations

Most of the temples are now linked together in countrywide associations. Their aim is to strengthen Hindus' sense of cultural and religious identity. The National Council of Hindu Temples (U.K.) is the best known. By 1983, thirty-two temples were affiliated to it. The Vishnu Hindu Parshad (U.K.) is another such organisation.

Other associations aim to preserve the cultural traditions of Hinduism. Local businessmen started some of them. They were keen to enhance their personal reputation by organising religious, charitable and cultural activities for the benefit of the local Hindu community. Others were organised by regional and national caste groups and sometimes based at a temple. Because Hindus perceive this as the fixed abode of the gods it gives the caste a religious centre and makes its activities objects of the god's grace. In Bradford

the 'Indian Association' was initially formed by
fifteen men representing families from several
different castes. However, despite its name, all
the members are Gujaratis.

The associations organise social, cultural and
religious events in which the ethnic and religious
identity of those who take part may be affirmed.
They oversee the celebration of festivals, provide
language classes where children can learn their
family's traditional Indian language, show Indian
films, teach yoga and Indian dance, and put on
performances of Indian music or other activities
of special interest to Hindus.

Self-help Unions

These emphasise character formation, self-reliance
and team effort. The members join in traditional
Indian games as well as other sports. These unions
often provide libraries of Indian books in Indian
languages as well as in English for the younger
generation. Their object is not so much to encourage specific Hindu religious practices as to uphold
the values of Hindu civilisation. Such organisations are numerous. In Bradford alone there
are nineteen different Hindu cultural, caste and
devotional organisations, as well as many secular groups such as the Indian Workers' Associations, Indian Women's Association, Indian Youth
Associations, oriental arts groups, etc. You could
ask a Hindu acquaintance if he belongs to any
such organisations and get him to tell you what
goes on at their meetings. If they invite you to

attend one of their activities do go if you possibly
can.

Greater unity of Beliefs and Practices than in India

In previous chapters we have noted the wide variety of beliefs and rituals practised by different
Hindus. However in Britain many Hindu groups
have made attempts to co-operate so that a temple
may attract as large a community as possible.
In Leeds, Gujarati and Punjabi Hindus pooled
resources to establish a temple where they could
both worship. But each regional group prefers its
specific procedures.

In other places where different regional groups
have established a common temple, they have
standardised their procedures of worship. These
are somewhat different from their separate regional
traditions yet still preserve what the leaders consider essential to the continuity of Hindu religious
life in an alien setting.

Another reason why the priest and members of
the community have standardised this complex
religion is to make it understandable to the non-
Hindu. They stress the well-known gods, such as
Rama and Krishna, and attempt to select the key
features and rituals from different areas. So particular religious beliefs have been subordinated
in the interests of the general good. They see
a unified system of beliefs as providing ethnic
identity for all Hindus and one way of preserving
the Hindu 'community'.

Attendance at Religious Ceremonies

In many Hindu communities in Britain attendance at religious ceremonies of all kinds is increasing. In India and East Africa people met their own family and caste daily in the business of living. They would worship at home and visit the temple individually when they felt like it. In Britain the pattern has changed. Hours of work do not allow for stopping in at the temple at will – there is less free time. Joint gatherings for worship and other religious and cultural events have become more usual. As many as 500 people may gather for life-cycle ceremonies. So the emphasis has changed. It used to centre on the gods in the home and temple. Now it centres on the community that worships the gods.

People are still sensitive about different families and castes worshipping together. So the emphasis in worship tends to be on hymn singing and the arati or offering of light. Here no one has to handle anything touched by anyone else so worshippers do not run the risk of being contaminated by people they consider inferior.

Many Hindus however, attend the temple infrequently for personal religious devotion, using their homes instead. They only attend the temple for festivals and special occasions and call in the priest in time of need. Some more westernised Hindus only share in religious activities on family occasions. But often when they have children they begin to take a more active interest in religion generally and share more frequently in the social and religious celebrations of their extended family.

Marriage

The largest gatherings in the Hindu community in Britain are for weddings. In Britain, churches and other buildings used for marriage ceremonies have to be licensed. In India there is no law requiring temples to be so registered. There is an immense variety of marriage forms which are locally and socially determined. The legality of a particular Hindu marriage is determined on the basis of community recognition. Common to most of them are the seven circles of seven steps round the sacred fire (p. 51).

In Britain, traditional Hindu laws have no standing, so all Hindus have to be married in a registry office to comply with British law. Hindus see marriage not as just two people giving and receiving promises, but as each extended family accepting the other. Thus they regard the registry office ceremony as a formality or possibly a betrothal. Many Hindus refer to it as the 'court' marriage. They often invite very few people to witness it. Afterwards the couple may continue to live in their respective homes and do not consummate the marriage. The 'real' marriage remains traditionally Hindu. It may take place several months after the 'court' marriage, last for several days and be attended by several hundred guests. Wedding anniversaries are counted from the date of the Hindu ceremony, though celebrations at such times are not part of Hindu tradition. In some cases nowadays, the registrar comes to the temple and carries out the civil formalities at the time of the Hindu wedding.

Hindu marriage rituals in Britain are usually

short by comparison with those in India. Families often ask the priest to abbreviate some of the rituals and abandon the less important ones. In India, priests will examine the couple's horoscopes to decide a favourable date for the marriage. In Britain weekends are the most convenient time for large ceremonies, and families often pressurise the priest to conduct them then, even if he considers the day is an unlucky one. Many priests adjust by agreeing to perform the marriage but point out that they can give no guarantee of its success when conducted on such a day.

The majority of Hindus realise that the registry office marriage is crucial to its legal recognition. They know they need a marriage certificate for tax purposes, all kinds of state benefits, immigration, travel abroad and other official paper work. However the older generation feel that the Hindu wedding is equally important because it helps to maintain Hindu culture in an alien environment.

The younger generation usually agree that both forms of marriage are valuable but are often not sure why. As far as the Hindu ceremony goes they enjoy the social occasion but may be less enthusiastic about the religious ceremony. Some complain that they don't understand the rituals. This is partly because they are conducted in Sanskrit, with which they are not familiar. Some Hindu priests, aware of this difficulty, give a running commentary in English, alongside the Sanskrit, to explain what they are doing.

Marriage instability is increasing among the younger generation of Hindus, though it is at present less critical than among white British couples. This is partly because couples often have not understood the promises they made.

Other ceremonies

As with marriage, most other Hindu ceremonies have undergone some adaptation on being transferred to Britain. There are many reasons for this. Most ceremonies in India and East Africa are held out of doors. Here when the weather is bad they have to be held in a building. Some Hindus worry about music and singing disturbing the neighbours. Often Hindu leaders have selected, modified and developed the traditions for the sake of preserving their identity and presenting a common front to non-Hindus. Such is the price their followers have paid in transferring to a new location.

Conflict between the generations

Most older Hindu people are concerned about maintaining the Hindu way of life in Britain and are anxious to transmit it to the younger generations. Conflict sometimes arises between Hindu parents and their adolescent children over morals and demands for independence. The parents often expect the youngsters to accept their traditions and values but do not explain why. This may be because the parents themselves have not been taught the meaning or do not have a very extensive knowledge of their religion. For them it has been enough to follow the traditions of their family and caste because they were so interwoven into their daily life when they were young. Some Hindu priests try to teach the younger generation but others just expect them to listen to readings without any explanations.

Hindus who have grown up in the West often experience conflicts with Western education. The pat answers their elders have taught them, that god is in everything, or that everything is maya (illusion), cause conflicts with the scientific teaching they receive at school.

What are the differences between Hindu and Christian attitudes to worship?

The Western concept of religion expects group religious activities to be performed in a consecrated building in the presence of ordained ministers. But Christians must not look for the values of the Hindu religion in similar ways. Hindus do not make a distinction between the private practice of the home and the public religious life of the temple. The Hindu home is conceived of as the abode of the gods. The women, especially, continue to fast and perform regular pujas there. Life-cycle rituals are usually celebrated in the home too, whereas Christian baptisms, communion and marriage take place in religious buildings.

Hindus consider rituals to be effective regardless of whether the performer understands them or not. Correct performance is what counts. When a divine word is uttered it is the sound, not the meaning, which is crucial.

In addition, the Westerner looks for fulfilment
in this life. The Hindu acknowledges that life is
incapable of fulfilment. The union of the individual soul with Brahman, some time in the far
distant future, is what matters.

Meaning and significance in Hinduism

In India many worshippers carry out their religious practices without questioning how and why.
They form a natural part of the fibre of everyday
life. Traditional Hindus see their religion as something into which a person is born, not something
into which he can convert. They feel, once a Hindu
always a Hindu. But in Britain, many of them are
becoming increasingly aware of their ignorance
about the meaning and content of their faith. They
meet people who question Hindu beliefs, practices
and values in a way they have never before come
across. When British friends ask them to explain
the meaning of their beliefs they are discovering
they cannot do so. This has led Hindu leaders to
teach the meaning and significance of many of the
rituals. The National Council of Hindu Temples
(U.K.) has published a booklet, 'An Introduction
to the World's Oldest Religion', in which they
clearly link Hinduism with the Indian way of
life and express their concern that it should be
understood by non-Hindus. They say, 'There is
little likelihood of harmony and integration for
an ethnic community unless its culture is understood and to some extent appreciated by the host
society.'[2]

The need for Hindus to understand the meaning

of their faith has also led to the development of a
fundamentalist movement, whose members insist
that Hindus should return to the doctrines and
practices of the Vedas and Upanishads. They are
prepared to use force when they think it necessary,
as they did at Ayodhya (p. 72). They are gaining
ground in Britain, as well as in India, and could
become as powerful as the fundamentalist party
in Islam.

Things to do

1. Ask a Hindu friend to tell you how he feels
   about arranged marriages.

2. Ask him how Indian parents go about arranging the marriages of their children. Talk about
   how different it is in Western culture and discuss the advantages and disadvantages of both
   approaches. But don't assume that all Hindus
   have arranged marriages.

3. If possible talk to a Hindu couple about their
   wedding. They may be able to show you photographs.

4. Find an opportunity to talk with Hindu parents you know well about their anxieties in
   bringing up children in a culture different from
   their own.

TEN
DISCUSSION WITH HINDUS

If you are going to share the message of Jesus with Hindus in a meaningful way you need to prepare yourself. Preparation takes time and effort but it is a small price to pay compared with what Jesus has done for us. Here are some suggestions of ways to do so.

Know the Bible

Read the Bible daily so that you grow in your ability to share God's truth. Learn by heart verses which help to explain the way to God. Most people love stories, so practise telling Bible stories in private and use them when the opportunity arises. Always have your Bible with you when visiting Hindus so that you can use it when appropriate ... avoid putting it on the floor as this implies that you don't respect it (p. 79).

Training Classes

If there are classes locally about reaching Hindus for Christ make sure you take part. If not ask your minister about organising some.

Pray

Prayer should underlie all our activity for God
and you should pray daily for your developing
friendships with Hindus. If you ask friends to
pray with or for you, be sure they are absolutely
trustworthy and discreet. Any gossip could destroy
your opportunities as well as damage people you
hope to lead to Christ.

Trust the Holy Spirit

Remember you are not on your own as you witness.
The Holy Spirit is with you to meet each situation,
guide every conversation and take you beyond
your natural abilities. You are only responsible
for witnessing. Convincing Hindus that the truth
is in Jesus is the Holy Spirit's responsibility.

Long-term involvement

A Hindu who comes to Christ makes an enormous
leap of faith in doing so. You may talk with an
interested Hindu many times before she is anywhere near ready to consider the claims of Christ
personally. We cannot expect her to appreciate in
a few weeks what most of us absorbed over the
years as we grew up.

Realise the cost of becoming
a Christian

A Hindu who comes to Christ and openly declares
her faith usually faces opposition from her family

and religious community. This will often take the
form of outright rejection. If her family throw her
out of the house a Christian family must take her
in – a new disciple will find it less of a culture
shock if she can live with an Asian Christian
family rather than a Western one.

A young person will find marriage a problem
as most marriages in Hindu society are arranged
by the family. They will usually pressurise her
to marry a Hindu, hoping to bring her back to
her former faith. Western Christians who know
a person in this situation must put aside any
pre-conceived ideas they have about arranged
marriages and do their best to help her to find
a Christian partner. Several Christian agencies
could help anyone needing advice about this (see
the Resources list at the back of the book).

Very often being a Christian in the West means
adapting to some extent to Western culture. We
do not realise how much our culture influences
the practice of our faith, but most new Asian
Christians find it a problem. Our insensitivity to
this can lead to their returning to their old faith.
If you have the opportunity to help a Christian
from a Hindu background do be sensitive to her
cultural as well as her spiritual difficulties.

Inviting a Hindu to church

You must be very careful how you do this –
never invite her as an easy way out of talking
to her personally about your Christian faith. You
should first establish a real friendship in which
she feels she can trust you before you issue such

an invitation. Even when she accepts she may find it difficult to worship in a Western style. The majority of Hindus do — though a few, especially the young, have become very Westernised and will not find it a problem. One Asian Christian, talking about the first time he attended church, said that he was upset at entering without taking off his shoes, and sitting on a chair instead of the floor. He felt he was being disrespectful to God. He added that six years after becoming a Christian it still hurts a little to behave as Westerners do in church. As a Hindu for whom alcohol was taboo he also found taking wine at communion difficult. Inviting a Hindu friend on a church outing, or to see a Christian film in the church hall, may be an easier first step. At first, they may also feel more at ease in a house group rather than the church.

Pray about the church to which you should introduce a potential disciple. Different styles of worship appeal to different people. Nisha was once fearful about her brother going to a Pentecostal church. She thought the service might be over-powering for him. But he loved the dancing and thought the worship was wonderful.

Have a genuine concern for Hindu friends and acquaintances

Ask God to enable you to act as Jesus did to the Samaritan woman he met at the well (John 4). He did not simply see her as a person to whom he could give his message. He showed real love and concern.

Points of Contact

Moral standards

In South Asia people are presumed to belong to one religious community or another. They think being British is equivalent to being a Christian and compare our present day standards of morality unfavourably with their own. This may seem negative, but if a Hindu friend expresses this thought to you suggest that she reads the New Testament to see the standards Jesus set.

Use straightforward English

Hindus for whom English is a second language know basic words and phrases but not idioms. However those who have been brought up and educated here have the same vocabulary as their peers. Always use plain English rather than religious jargon.

Pray for and with your friends

Your efforts to win Hindus for Christ will be fruitless unless you pray for them. Prayer is far more important than skilful talking about the Christian faith. When the opportunity arises tell them that Christians believe worship and prayer should be part of one's daily life. Hindus revere their gods to whom they offer love, prayers and sacrifice so they understand about loving God and worshipping him. Most of them will be happy for you to pray with them and doing so will show that you care. If a Hindu with whom you have contact seems interested in the gospel try to get the names of his family members and their relationships and pray for them. Whole extended families have come to Christ because Christians did so.

Some warnings

Don't pressurise a Hindu to accept Christ

Some Hindu friends love to please. In fact they consider it impolite to give a negative answer to a question. If they profess faith in Christ out of politeness this can hinder them from coming into a true relationship with him at a later date.

Don't seem patronising

You must never imply that you feel superior because you are white or even because you are a Christian. Even shyness can be misinterpreted as aloofness. If you are shy and find it hard to talk to strangers bring your problem to the Lord in prayer. He can give the most reserved person courage if they are willing to step out in faith.

Don't run down their religion

Hindus value their own heritage. Instead of telling them what is wrong with their faith, emphasise the positive help you find in Christianity. *Ask* a Hindu what his scriptures say, don't *tell*. Remember that you are not an authority on Hinduism but someone with an understanding of the Bible which you can share with your Hindu friend. Never be disrespectful to Hinduism when talking with an Asian, it won't get you anywhere.

Don't be afraid to admit you don't know all the answers

When you don't know the answer to a question a Hindu asks, say you will try to find out. If you can't do so, admit your ignorance. But share the

joy and peace of trusting God for what we don't
understand.

Don't get involved in philosophical discussion

Asians will talk about the philosophical aspects
of religion as readily as British people discuss
the weather or different brands of soap powder.
But it usually leads nowhere as far as sharing
the reality of Christ is concerned. If they bring
up some philosophical matter try to draw them
back to the basics of the gospel. A Hindu once
asked Rani what would happen to all the people
in the third world who had never heard about
Jesus. Rani simply said, 'Your first duty is to
watch out for your own soul.' She brought her
back to the matter of her personal relationship
with God, rather than abstract objections, and
she became a follower of Jesus Christ.

The Death of Christ

Though Hindus do not see Jesus as unique, they
appreciate his death on the cross as a symbol of
self-denial. They are also drawn to the Christian
who denies himself for the sake of God and other
people. Your conduct is more important than
thousands of words of preaching.

Sharing your testimony

If you talk about God, Hindus will want to know
how he has worked in your life. This will impress
them far more than any explanation of Christian

theology. You can also tell them how God has answered your prayers, guided you, saved you from mistakes or changed your attitudes. But don't go on and on about your experiences. Most people switch off when you do. Think through the really important parts of your Christian experience and practise telling it in five minutes. This will help both you and your Hindu friend to see what really matters.

It is important not to rely only on answers to prayer or miracles in your testimony because many Hindus who follow gurus will simply counter with miracles their own gurus are supposed to have performed, or prayers they have answered. We follow Christ because he died for our sins and no guru has ever done that.

Avatars, reincarnations of one of the gods, usually Vishnu, have never atoned for sins. They are not God in the flesh. They are simply aspects of the Hindu gods, never the total incarnation of every aspect of divinity. Only in Christ is the fullness of God revealed. No Hindu scripture can dispute this.

Following Krishna, for example, is only following one aspect of one god in one form; but Christ's incarnation brought the totality of God into our physical world.

What practical aids to witnessing are there?

The Bible and Scripture portions
Not many enquirers will want to receive an entire Bible but most will accept a Gospel. The Bible

Society publishes Gospels in all the languages common to Hindus in Britain. Scripture Gift Mission produces selections of Scriptures for free distribution. All Rani's family were initially introduced to Scripture through the *Daily Strength* booklet, published by the Scripture Gift Mission. When they later heard the gospel, for the first time, in church, some of the verses were already familiar.

Other Christian literature

The Foreign Literature Department of the Christian Literature Crusade (CLC) holds stocks of most literature suitable for Hindus in Britain. They include tracts, stories of people of their own background who have come to Christ, and simple explanations of Christian truths.

Cassettes

These days many people do not read much and some older Hindus may be illiterate. The only way to reach them is through the spoken word. Language Recordings International has a wide selection of suitable tapes. Many tapes of Christian songs in Asian languages are also on the market, produced by Kingsway with South Asian Concern.

Videos

Most Hindu families in Britain own a video recorder and there are a number of Christian video films useful for evangelism. For an extensive list contact either South Asian Concern, PO Box 43, Sutton, Surrey SM2 5WL or your local Christian Bookshop.

Witnessing together with others.

Not all evangelistic activity is done on an individual basis. If you worship in an area where there are Hindus encourage your minister and elders to organise some outreach activities. These can include: door-to-door visiting, distribution of literature, and open air services. For the latter, the witnessing group should be multi-racial and some singing and preaching should be in a local Asian language, if possible. You could also have bookstalls at public events such as carnivals and shows. Some churches have arranged an evangelistic mission to Hindus in the area, with an outside team helping. But this is only worthwhile if local Christians are willing to commit themselves to follow-up afterwards.

What of holiday clubs for children? These are happy experiences for most children. However you must be careful not to pressurise those from Hindu families to accept Christ and go home and tell the family. Their parents will probably then forbid them to attend any Christian activity. You can help the children to appreciate how much Jesus loves them and leave the suggestion of making a decision until they are mature enough to stand up to pressure. However, you may find some children taking such a step even though you have not mentioned it. If so it is vitally important that you maintain strict confidentiality.

You can also build on Christian festivals. At times like Christmas and Easter some Asians are willing to come to a celebration which includes an explanation of the festival or a drama, plus music. A procession through the streets of your local area at the time of a festival is another way of drawing people's attention to it. If several churches can join together for this it can make a special impact.

Some of Santosh's relations came to the Lord in times of crisis. Others had difficulty choosing between Christ and a guru. Santosh got them to compare whatever choice of guru they wanted to make with the way of Christ. His family members and Asian friends have held beliefs that range from Zoroastrianism to Islam, but Santosh always maintained contact with them in spite of their different beliefs. Eventually he was able to talk with them further and many of them have now accepted Christ. Never burn your bridges too soon.

For Santosh keeping up links and constant prayer were a priority. Presenting Christ as culturally relevant to them was also important, as well as emphasising that Christ paid the price for our sins thus removing any need for reincarnations.

Hindus come to the Lord in many different ways. This is Dilip and Neeta's testimony:

Dilip and Neeta's story

Dilip begins

I was born in Tanzania where I went to a
Roman Catholic school. I knew the people
there worshipped Jesus and I saw a cross.
   When I was eighteen I came to England.
I found work in a factory. I often thought
I would like to know Jesus for myself. One

night he came to me in a dream. When I
told my relatives about it they laughed at
me. But from that day I was different and
believed in Jesus. Each day as I went to
work on the bus we passed many churches.
I felt I wanted to go in but never did.

Then one day a neighbour, a young Asian
from Fiji, gave me a Bible and talked to me
a lot about Jesus. Then he moved and we
lost touch with each other. But I began to
read the Bible before I went to bed. One
night I read that Jesus would come again
and I asked, 'Lord, are you coming again
as a baby? And which place are you going
to come to?' That night I had a dream. I
saw him coming again on the clouds. At
that time I hadn't read 1 Thessalonians but
when I did it was just like my dream. The
next day when I went to work I was totally
changed. I stopped smoking, drinking, and
all my old bad habits.

Then I started looking for a church where
I could worship Jesus. One day I heard a
man preaching in the market place. After
he had finished preaching I went up to him
and said, 'I believe in Jesus. I want to go to
church.'

That evening he brought an Indian
Christian, from a Hindu background, to my
house. The next Sunday I went to church
with him.

One day I heard that my mother had
found a girl for me to marry. So I went
home to Tanzania for the occasion.

Before our wedding I told Neeta, 'I

worship Jesus and I don't want to get
married in the Hindu way. And when we're
married I don't want any burning of lights
to gods in my house.'

But, at the wedding, my family forced me
to go through the Hindu ceremony and to
worship the images. But, as I did so, I said
in my heart, 'Lord Jesus, I'm going through
all these things. Forgive me. I'm standing
in front of the images but I'm talking to
you, not them.' When I returned to Britain
I felt sorry I'd not been brave enough to
stand out against my relatives.

My wife was willing to come to church
with me. I kept telling her that the Lord
forgave me for all my past sins. The Lord
has taught me a lot about forgiveness.
Jesus has forgiven me not once but every
day. But the most important thing is that
Jesus loves you and died for you on the
Cross.

Neeta takes up the story

Before our marriage Dilip told me he didn't
want lights burning before images in his
house and I said, 'That's fine'. My
background was strongly Hindu but it was
sometimes a hindrance to me. I prayed
and got no answers and didn't know why. I
fasted because I was taught that if I prayed,
fasted and sacrificed before the images
God would give me what I asked. But that
never satisfied me, so I didn't mind what
Dilip said.

I went to a Roman Catholic school in

India, though my parents lived in Tanzania.
So I knew what the Roman Catholics
believed, but thought, 'That's their
religion'. When Dilip told me his personal
experience of the Lord I said to myself,
'That's something different. It's not the
same as the Roman Catholics told me.
They used to tell us Hinduism was a good
religion to follow too.'

When I reached England I went to church
with Dilip but didn't think I should give my
life to Jesus.

Within a few months I found I was
expecting a baby. After some scans one
day, the doctor said, 'We think the baby
has spina bifida. We would like to abort it.'
I said, 'I'd like that.' But when I told Dilip
he said, 'No, my God won't do that. He will
look after us.'

So as not to upset Dilip, I agreed to carry
on with the baby. After a few weeks I had
another scan. Afterwards doctors, nurses,
and a specialist, five people in all, came
into the room. I thought, 'It must be very
serious for them all to come at once.' Then
the doctor said, 'We're glad to say that
there's nothing wrong with your child.' I
said, 'Praise Jesus! Praise Jesus!' It just
came out. Then the doctor said, 'It's unreal.
Let's go and congratulate your husband.
Your God is a miracle-working God.' And he
is, it's true.

When we had the news about the baby
having spina bifida an Asian Christian
friend had said, 'We'll pray for you. Don't

worry.' And they did. Though I didn't tell
Dilip, I had said in my heart, 'Jesus, if you
are really alive, please save my baby.' When
I knew everything was all right I said,
'Lord, you *are* my Saviour. You saved my
child and me. I ask your forgiveness.' From
that day I accepted the Lord Jesus.

One thing I never forget. One day an
Asian Christian friend was praying for
the baby in my womb. He always said, 'By
Jesus' precious blood.' I remembered that
when I gave my life to Jesus. I said, 'Lord
Jesus, I know you died for me and made me
clean with your precious blood.' This is not
in Hinduism. None of the gods died for me.
None of the gods shed their blood for me.
This really hit me and still sticks with me.

In Hinduism you just talk to an image
and it's just made of stone. But God is alive,
listening to you and he really appreciates
your praise. We can have a real relationship
with God, our Father. In Hinduism
everything is dead. In Christianity
everything is alive.

Things to do

1. If you do not already have a Hindu friend, get
   to know someone of that religion in the ways
   suggested in Chapter Two.

2. Ask your friend to tell you how she practises
   her faith. For example does she worship at
   the local temple? Does she have a shrine in

her own home? Does she read any particular
holy books or say particular prayers? Listen
carefully and ask friendly questions as the
conversation proceeds.

3. Ask your friend if you may pray with her for any
   special needs she may have. Ask her to suggest
   what posture you should you use – standing,
   sitting, kneeling.

4. Decide what are the important parts of your
   testimony. Write it out so that it takes no
   longer than 5 minutes to tell. If possible tell
   it to a Christian friend and ask for her reaction
   before sharing it with Hindus.

5. Get some copies of the Scripture Gift Mission
   booklet Daily Strength to give to your Hindu
   friends. They also have a wide range of useful
   booklets in many Asian languages.

6. If your Hindu friends read English give them
   copies of the biographies in the book list at the
   back of the book.

ELEVEN

COMMON HINDU OBJECTIONS TO CHRISTIANITY

Introduction

Evangelising Hindus in the West is different from doing so in India. Western culture is less hospitable for Hinduism to prosper in than India. There, the accumulated weight of 4,000 years of Hindu culture and tradition opposes the Christian who tries to share his faith.

At the same time the Church in India can teach us much about how to reach Hindus with the gospel. The following statement by the East Asia Christian Conference applies to Britain as well as to Asia:

A living theology must speak to the actual questions men are asking in the midst of their dilemmas; their hopes; their aspirations and achievements; their doubts, despair and suffering. It must also speak in relation to the answers that are being given by Asian religions and philosophies, both in their classical form and in new forms

created by the impact on them of Western
thought, secularism and science. Christian
theology will fulfil its task (among Hindus)
only as the churches, as servants of God's
Word and revelation in Jesus Christ, speak
to the Asian situation and from involvement
in it.

The ultimate aim in evangelising is not to make
people change from one religion to another. That
is futile. Religion never saved anyone – only Christ
can do that. The weakest point in establishing a
relationship between Christ and our Hindu neighbours is *ourselves*. The strongest is Christ himself.
Neither are 'joining the church' or 'meeting other
Christians' satisfactory goals when encouraging
a Hindu to search for the true God. We have
to distinguish between them meeting Christ the
person and meeting Christians. One Asian Christian sometimes says, when preaching, "Meeting
Christ was exciting. The problems set in when I
met Christians . . . It got worse with Christianity,
and Churchianity blew it.'

As a general guide be careful with the use of
terms and ensure that they are understood clearly.
If the Hindu is arguing from the belief that there
is no absolute truth, even the words he uses can
have a variety of interpretations and shades of
meaning.

You should not let yourself be dragged into arguments. Jesus refused to argue with the Samaritan
woman (John 4) when she asked him if he was
greater than Jacob. He simply told her that he
would give her a life that was eternally satisfying.
Of course, you will want to discuss matters your

Hindu friend brings up, but never ridicule him and his beliefs, talk down to him or show annoyance.

When speaking to a Hindu about your faith, and especially when trying to counter objections to the gospel, remember that the key issues usually revolve around the uniqueness of Christ. Make sure you understand and can defend this position or you will flounder. If your Hindu friend asks a question, paraphrase it back to him to make sure you really know what he is asking. Hinduism teaches that there are many ways to God. In the end only the Holy Spirit can convince a Hindu that Jesus is the only way. Prayer for him to do so is a crucial part of any witnessing to such people.

Sharing the gospel message with Hindus is challenging. There are difficulties to overcome, misunderstandings to clear up, prejudices to remove and suspicions to allay. But if you depend on the Holy Spirit he can help you in all these. Here are some common reactions you will meet.

All ways lead to God

When we first meet a Hindu he will object if we say that Jesus is the only way and accuse us of being narrow-minded and arrogant. Argument will not persuade him otherwise. Let your attitude show humble thankfulness that Christ revealed himself to you, so the charge of arrogance will not stick.

Hindus see no reason to change their faith because they believe they are born Hindus and should remain so. Most Hindus have no missionary vision because they think it does not matter what spiritual path we follow, that we are all on the way to God. If you challenge them on this point they will probably tell you that Hindus have believed this for generations and many millions of people can't be wrong. But this argument is invalid. After all, millions believed the earth was flat until it was proved otherwise.

You need to counter the objection by explaining what Christ said – not that Christianity is *a*, or even *the* way – but that *he himself* is the true and living way and that no one comes to God except through him.

There is no absolute truth

Hinduism teaches that truth is different for different people in different situations. You will usually find Hindus reluctant to accept that truth is always the same and that God's standards are set for all people and all time. The only way you can effectively help is by praying for the Holy Spirit to show them.

We believe the same as you

Because Hinduism has no systemised set of beliefs, no one is branded an unbeliever. Their attitude of treating all religions alike makes it difficult to argue with Hindus.

Some of them are attracted by certain Christian ideas and incorporate them into their own belief system. But this does not mean they are accepting the entire Christian message. Christians need to present clearly but sensitively that our salvation stands or falls, not on ideas, but on a personal relationship with Jesus.

The story of Jesus is just another legend

Hindus do not distinguish clearly between history and legend. For Christians the fact that Jesus was a real flesh and blood man who lived in Palestine at a dated time is important. A Hindu sees little difference between the stories of Krishna and Rama (which seem legendary to us) and those about Jesus. However, the stories of the former grew from literary origins whereas those of Jesus are based on the accounts of actual eye witnesses. Even so eternal truths appear more important to educated Hindus than once and for all historical events. This makes it difficult for us to convey the uniqueness of Christ's incarnation as a real event and not merely a story with a moral.

We worship Christ too

Since Hindus believe that all ways lead to God, they usually admire Jesus as a great teacher. They also approve of Christians who try to follow him. They will accept the idea that Jesus is a god but not that he is the only way to the one true God. Hindus are often happy to worship him alongside their own gods, but not to give him pride of place.

Christians treat wrongdoing too lightly

The Hindu understanding of sin is in the doctrine
of karma. It teaches that everyone must suffer
for their sins. Not even God can give him a free
pardon. This is so deeply rooted in the minds of
Hindus that it blinds them to the truth that Jesus
died on the Cross for every human being. It seems
to them that Christians think they can do wrong
and get away with it scot-free. We have to explain
that Jesus took all the punishment for sin that
should have been ours and that God is a just judge
and no judge punishes twice for the same offence.
So all who trust in what Jesus has done for them
are freed from any penalty and receive the gift of
eternal life. You may have to go over this several
times before they are able to grasp what you are
trying to say. Hindus see acceptance by God not
as a matter of trusting him, but of struggling
to do good deeds in order to win his approval.
Salvation does not occur here and now as the
Christian believes but only after an individual
has experienced countless births and deaths. It
may be many thousands of years in the future.
Before asking a Hindu to accept Christ you must
make sure he fully understands that he needs a
Saviour and that he can only find him in Jesus.

Christianity is a Western religion

This statement again assumes that there are
many ways to truth and many bridges to God.

Hindus often assume that Jesus is for white people and Hinduism is for them. This error is also found in some sections of the church community. They see religion as a matter of birth rather than choice.

In South Asia everyone is assumed to be of some religion or other. So 80 per cent of Indians consider themselves Hindus, and the majority of Pakistanis, Muslim. Children born in Britain to Hindu parents are also expected to be Hindus. Similarly they expect all Westerners to be Christians.

With the exception of the Syrian Church in South India, Christianity was brought to India by white missionaries. Indians assumed their religion was part of their cultural baggage. Because missionaries were active during the days of British imperialism most Hindus equate Christianity with foreign domination. Those who have been born since independence have picked up this idea from their parents and grandparents, even if they were born outside India.

Jesus has usually been portrayed in Western art, literature and song as having white skin, fair hair and blue eyes. This again gives Hindus the message that Jesus is Western and probably middle class too. You can help to correct this misapprehension by pointing out that Jesus lived all his life in the Middle East and that his lifestyle was Asian rather than European. Thomas, one of his apostles, is reputed to have set up a church in South India. Whether this is true or not, we do know there has been a Syrian Church in South India since the second century AD. So Christianity reached India before it came to Britain.

Christians are intolerant

You need to be very sensitive in witnessing to Hindus. One Christian said, 'I wouldn't know how to tell them what is wrong with their religion.' Homing in like this on the aspects of their religion you consider faulty is to be avoided. You should not condemn their beliefs or practices. This will alienate them. Let them be drawn by the love of Christ and his sacrifice on the Cross.

Men like Paul the apostle, and Martin Luther came to Christ out of a sense of need not because they had discovered that Christianity was better than all other religions. It is wise to confine yourself to talking about how Jesus can meet all our needs rather than argue about the superiority of Christianity over Hinduism. Your approach should never be patronising but humble and loving. Paul, the righteous and blameless Pharisee, said he was the chief of sinners Jesus came to save. How much more should we be humble in telling Hindus about Christ.

We don't approve of the Christian lifestyle

Some Hindus, especially the younger generation, are attracted by aspects of Western culture which they mistakenly label Christian. These include music, customs, social consciousness etc. Others are repelled by Western ideas and morals. When they appear to reject the gospel, they may really be rejecting the Western lifestyle in which it is presented.

Older Hindus in Britain view our permissive society with distaste. In their culture opposite sexes do not talk to each other in public let alone show affection. Respectable women dress discreetly. They consider the dress of many British women immodest and provocative. The open presentation of sex in the media offends them. Because they assume all white people are Christians this gives them the impression that the moral standards of Christianity are low. A Christian who makes friends with Hindus needs to explain that much behaviour in British society today does not reflect Christian standards. Their own conduct must of course affirm what they say. If a Hindu friend brings up this topic of the Christian life style you may be able to suggest that he reads the New Testament to see the standards Jesus set.

Most Hindus consider animal life sacred and so are vegetarians. The fact that most Christians eat meat can be a major stumbling block for Hindus. They find it difficult to believe that Christians can eat animals and talk about loving God at the same time. For them loving God means not killing what he has created.

Hindus sometimes point to the long list of wars in the West and to the prevalence of racism as a condemnation of Christianity. This again illustrates their mistake in assuming that anything Western reflects Christian teaching. You need to explain to Hindu friends that true Christians condemn these just as they do.

Don't start a friendship with a Hindu by inviting him to a Western church. In addition to what we have said in Chapter Ten, you should realise that he will probably be put off by receiving three or four unfamiliar books and be further embarrassed as everybody else flicks confidently through them. Most Hindu worshippers know their hymns and prayers by heart. Also the rhythm and harmonies of English music sound strange to their ears.

If Hindus meet together for worship, men sit on one side of the room and women on the other. Your friend will be upset to see men and women sitting together indiscriminately; and may be particularly shocked to see young people of opposite sexes talking freely to each other, especially if they hold hands or express affection in any way. He may well feel that what is going on cannot be worship. A Hindu over the age of thirty will be particularly sensitive about this. Students usually have a more open attitude.

If there is an Asian Christian Fellowship in your area consider introducing him there rather than to your church. If you don't know of one locally, you can consult the agencies listed at the back of the book.

Christians take young people away from their families

Most of us are aware that some sects, such as the Moonies, separate young people from their families. But some Hindus whose young people have become mainstream Christians feel the same about the Church. Because of the close-knit nature of the extended family any member who acts out of line or questions its activities or views is considered a traitor. They also assume that if he becomes a Christian he will become totally

Western, take an English name and forget all about them. The family will suffer a great deal of pain from his supposed betrayal. In addition, in India, those converted from Hinduism have been largely from low caste groups, so most older Hindus despise Christians. Anyone from a high caste Hindu family who becomes one loses his caste status, and this is a great grief for his relatives.

A young person from a Hindu family who becomes a Christian may be turned out of his home. (p. 121) However, you should urge him to remain faithful to the family in every way possible. The love of Jesus shown in a believer's life can overcome persecution. In many cases the persistent demonstration of this love has meant that that young person has, in the end, become the most trusted son or daughter.

It is difficult to win older people, especially fathers and grandfathers, to Christ. But this does not mean that we shouldn't try. When a young person becomes a Christian those in contact with him should make a point of praying regularly for his extended family. In one instance, this resulted in over twenty of them turning to Jesus. If the head of a family becomes a Christian the rest will often follow. So prayer for him is particularly important.

Share Christ not Christianity

When sharing the gospel with Hindus, introduce them, not to another way of reaching God, but to God himself. He is the ultimate goal of all longings and strivings. Allow them to meet Christ

and let everything else be a separate issue. Let a
Hindu become a 'follower of Christ' rather than
'a Christian'. It's all the same to us but a less
threatening concept to a Hindu.

Things to do

1. When you next spend time with a Hindu friend
   ask him to tell you which parts of his faith are
   most important to him. Listen carefully to what
   he says and think about which things you could
   also accept. It will usually be right for you in
   turn to tell about what is important to you.

2. At your next meeting start to talk about beliefs
   which you have in common. Then gently introduce some of those over which you differ. Be
   very gracious about how you do so. Do not get
   into an argument.

3. Listen to any criticisms he may have about
   Christians. If they are a result of misunderstanding try to clear these up. Don't lose your
   temper or criticise Hindus in return.

4. Set aside times to pray for your Hindu friend
   especially bearing in mind the things that have
   come to light in your talks.

5. Have a role-play session between yourself and
   another Christian to explore the uniqueness of
   Christ. Let one defend the idea and the other
   challenge it. After the first role-play switch
   sides. Then you each have a chance to try
   presenting the gospel and also the Hindu's
   arguments.

TWELVE

EXPLAINING THE GOSPEL

At one time Sohan worked in the City of London for an international bank. Many of the students in his foreign currency department had to complete a one day course on detecting counterfeit currency. Most of the time was taken up, not with examining bogus bank notes, but with looking at real currency.

The teacher explained that, once his students had handled and knew real currency inside out, they would be able to detect any counterfeits immediately.

Similarly with the gospel message, we should spend most of our time studying our own Bible, knowing our own Lord and exploring our own Church's teaching. Then, when it comes to sharing it, we will instantly know from the feedback we receive whether our listener has inadvertently misunderstood or if we accidently sold short the message of salvation. We will be able to detect the shades of variation between the teachings of gurus and the truth of Jesus Christ.

When explaining the gospel to a Hindu you don't have to become a good Hindu yourself. You just have to be a well-informed Christian, walking closely with God, and open to the opportunities

that the Holy Spirit will present. Once those
opportunities arise, don't try to impress your
Hindu friend with how much you've learnt about
his or her religion. Instead, concentrate on talking
about the aspects of Christianity which are likely
to lead into good fruitful conversations. Here are
some tips for doing so:

1 – What to concentrate on

Start with similarities

Religions have certain things in common and certain things that are different. To ignore the differences is not fair, but nor is it fair to over-
emphasise the differences and minimise or ignore
the similarities. The similarities between Hinduism
and Christianity can be bridges by which you can
gain a sympathetic hearing.

Most Hindus, despite their worship of many
gods, believe there is one absolute force behind
the whole of creation.

Most of them revere one of the gods, usually
Rama or Krishna. They offer him love and adora-
tion, so they will understand when you talk about
loving God and worshipping him. They will also
agree that prayer is important.

Hinduism has a tradition of holy men who
devote themselves to a life of poverty, prayer
and sacrifice. So Hindus are drawn to Jesus and
his death on the cross as a symbol of self-denial.

They are also drawn to the Christian who denies
himself for the sake of God and other people. A life
in which self-sacrifice is evident will say more than
thousands of words of preaching.

Hindus believe in the spiritual nature of human

beings and are therefore easier to talk to about God than many English people. They will also identify with your sharing your personal experience of him. They long for this themselves.

Use the Bible

You must make it clear that the Bible is the final authority in all matters relating to God. Hindus are used to the idea of following the teachings of a human guru. Explain that all Christian teaching must be in line with the Bible.

When you have talked to a Hindu about Jesus, it is good to give her a gospel and ask her to study the life and claims of Jesus. John's Gospel is the best one, because its mystical approach appeals to the Hindu way of thinking. Suggest that as she reads it she should make notes of anything that puzzles her. You can then discuss it next time you meet.

Be sure that you too study your Bible daily, so that you can use it easily when talking with a Hindu. Here are some scriptures which are particularly helpful.

1 Peter 1:19	The purity of Christ's life.
John 14:6	Jesus is the only way to God.
Romans 12:1	Christ does not want us to offer any sacrifice except that of our own lives.
Romans 3:23	Men and women are basically sinful.
Ephesians 2:8-9	We are not accepted by God
Titus 3: 5	because of what we do but by the free gift of his grace.
1 Timothy 2: 5	Man has a separate identity from God.

2 Timothy 3: 16 The Bible is inspired by God.
Hebrews 9: 27   We have only one life on earth.
John 14: 16-17 The Holy Spirit gives us the
         power to live as God requires.

Telling some of the parables and incidents in the life of Christ is also most effective. The Hindu scriptures are full of stories which many Hindus love. Often the stories in the gospels convey the truth much more effectively than abstract points.

Tell them about the Holy Spirit

Hindus spend their lives trying to gain good standing in God's sight. You can share the good news that, after we have accepted Jesus as our Saviour, he gives us his Holy Spirit who provides us with the power to do those things that please God. We do not have to struggle on our own.

Avoid Christian jargon

Many of us are so used to the jargon talked in Christian circles that we do not realise that people of other faiths interpret the words differently. Being 'born again' speaks to a Hindu of a continuous cycle of deaths and rebirths. 'Sin' to a Hindu means breaking caste rules or not performing religious rites correctly. So in discussion with a Hindu avoid technical terms altogether. For example, instead of using the word 'sins', talk about specifics such as telling lies, hurting people or thinking wrong thoughts. Instead of talking about 'being saved', explain the meaning of the Cross in simple language.

 Don't tell a Hindu that she must born again. She will either think you are telling her about

reincarnation, as though it were a teaching of
the church, or that you are telling her that she
is 'once born' – an outcaste – the lowest of the
low. The higher castes are known as 'twice born'.
Which ever way she takes it, you are going to
have a difficult task back-tracking and making
amends for the misunderstanding or offence you
have caused.

You should be careful about using such a phrase
as 'Jesus lives in me'. This is biblical, but confus-
ing to a Hindu. She thinks of humans as *being
God*, and of herself as a person trying to realise
this. Christians think of *being in communion with
God* but having a separate human identity.

In short, think through beforehand what Christian jargon you are accustomed to using. Then find
a way to express what you mean in simple English
instead.

Demonstrate Jesus in your daily life

Hindus are attracted to Christ by his life of un-
selfish love and sacrifice. The lives of Christians
who profess to be his disciples should also show
these virtues. The Christian who puts the welfare
of other people before his own will win more
Hindus to Christ than one who lives for his own
personal ease and comfort. This cannot be stressed
strongly enough. Be careful, however, that you
don't give the impression that the Christian life
is simply about doing good deeds. Hindus do that.
Many put Christians to shame.

Tell them how you pray

This will show that your concern for your fellow
human beings is rooted in your relationship with

God. Otherwise a Hindu may assume your concern is just a result of your own initiative. Pray with her when the opportunity arises. A simply worded personal prayer will be more effective than a long traditionally patterned one. She will be challenged by the personal relationship which is demonstrated. Be careful not to be condemning in what you pray. And do not preach – pray!

2 – Explaining words and concepts

Emphasise that God is a person
A Hindu tends to think of God, or Brahman, as an unknowable and impersonal force. You can tell her that God is personal and even list his attributes – his absolute purity, his power, his holiness, his everlasting love and so on. Show her that Jesus was an actual person, the events of whose life and death are recorded in history. Most Hindus will understand that you love and worship him. They themselves follow the path of bhakti, that is love and worship of their gods. And they think of them as personal, even though they may believe Brahman is impersonal.

The origin of life
Hinduism teaches that life is an endless cycle of births and deaths. You can agree that God is never-ending and share the biblical account of creation. This tells us he always was and always will be. Then you can say that the Bible teaches that our individual lives do have a beginning and an end and that one day God's whole creation, as we know it, will cease to exist.

The Christian concept of eternal life

Just to say to a Hindu that God promises eternal life is not enough. Hinduism teaches that living for ever is something from which to escape. Ask your friend what he believes will happen to him after death. Then go on to explain what Christ offers. Tell the story of the resurrection. Follow this by explaining that Jesus' resurrection offers us the hope of living with him in heaven. We don't merge with a supreme spirit like a drop in the ocean, but enjoy God for ever as his children. This explanation is crucial. One of the attractions of Christ to a Hindu is that he offers a personal relationship with God in this life and a clear hope after death.

The meaning of 'sin'

Hindus will understand when you talk about the emptiness of the human soul, the apparent lack of purpose in life, a sense of guilt and the longing for peace. Many of them experience such feelings. Do not tell them in a superior way that you have the answers. Come alongside them in humility and love and share about times when you have felt these things.

From this, tackle the root of sinfulness. Most Hindus think of sin as breaking the rules laid down in their holy books. They rarely realise it as disobedience to God. The concept that sin came into the world through the disobedience of man is hard for them to understand. They need to grasp that sin means we are separated from God: that we sin because we are sinners. They also need to understand that sin includes such things as dishonesty, unloving attitudes to others, wrong

thoughts etc., and not just breaking rules. Do not
go on to tell them that Jesus is the answer until
you have established the fact that they are in need
of deliverance from their own personal sin.

Salvation from sin is found only in Jesus

When your Hindu friend recognises her need of
forgiveness, you can then tell her how you found
the answer in Jesus. It will not be easy for her to
grasp this. Very deeply embedded in the minds
of Hindus is the doctrine of karma – that the
consequences of sin will be reaped when the soul
is reborn in another body. However this does mean
that a Hindu has no illusions about easy forgiveness. She may appreciate Paul's question in
Romans 3, 'How can God be both just and forgive
the sinner?' You can explain that he could only do
so by taking the karma of the world on himself. He
did this in the sacrifice of Christ on the Cross for
the sin of the world. This deliverance is a free gift
from God. He alone can save us from the endless
consequences of our karma. This usually seems
like cheap forgiveness to Hindus. They may feel
that if you are easily forgiven you will repeat the
same sin. You need to explain how God helps us
not to sin and how loving him means choosing not
to sin. You may have to repeat this on numerous
occasions. In the end only prayer will open their
eyes to the truth.

Jesus is unique

We have pointed out several times already that
Hindus object to the idea that Jesus is the only
way to God. When a Hindu does declare her faith

in Jesus make sure she understands that this
means forsaking all other gods and following only
Christ. Emphasise that he is the incarnation of the
one Creator God.

The doctrine of the Trinity

If a Hindu has heard of this she may be puzzled.
Does it mean we worship three gods? Why did
Jesus pray to God if he was God? Maybe you could
use the illustration of steam, water and ice as
different, yet the same. Or the fact that a man can
be husband, father and son simultaneously. The
three characteristics are in no way contradictory,
but add to the overall understanding of what we
are describing. Similarly the three persons of the
Trinity taken together give us a more complete
idea of the Godhead than each on his own.

   If a Hindu asks you questions of any sort which
you cannot answer, admit it. Then tell her you
will try to find out. Consult your minister or an
experienced Christian about what to say, before
you see that person again.

3 Some practical approaches

The keys to reaching a Hindu for Christ are
prayer, patience and persistence. Most Christians
learned their faith over many years. Do not expect
a Hindu to grasp its essentials in one or two
meetings. She may never have opened a Bible,
let alone know anything about its teaching. You
will need to build up a relationship of trust before
you can expect her to give you her confidence
or consider seriously what you say about your

beliefs. Maybe you will not speak much about
them the first few times you meet. You will be
concentrating on making friends. But as you do
so she will be noticing your behaviour and forming
her impressions of what Christians are like. You
need to stay close to God so that what you say and
do brings glory to him.

Here are some methods of sharing the gospel
which you may be able to use.

The Bible and Scripture portions

In Isaiah 55:11 we read '. . . the word that I
speak – it will not fail to do what I plan for it;
it will do everything I send it to do.' You cannot
over-estimate the power of the word of God to
speak to the hearts of men and women. Carry a
small copy of the Bible wherever you go, so that
you can read important verses or passages to your
Hindu friends.

But God's word does not depend on our presence
for its impact. It is powerful in itself. God will
speak to the heart of anyone who reads it with a
sincere desire to understand. Pray for any Hindu
to whom you have given a portion of Scripture.

Remember that not many people will want to
receive an entire Bible at first but most of them
will accept a gospel. Find out whether they prefer
to read in English or their own Asian language. At
the end of this book you will find addresses from
which you can obtain these.

Other Christian literature

Many Hindus are happy to receive reading material.
They often enjoy Christian biographies. Before
giving them any book be sure to read it yourself.

The spoken word

Though many Hindus are well educated there are others for whom reading, even of their first language, is not easy. But you can use the spoken word effectively. Many of the Bible narratives were first spoken and passed from one generation to another and only later written down. So other means of communication beside the written word are useful. These can include music, drama, poetry, videos, paintings, visual objects etc. Hindu friends will often be ready to accept invitations to events which include these before they want to come to a church service.

Inviting people to church

Bear in mind the warnings on pages 121 and 143. When you do feel it is appropriate, invite them to a special service, like Christmas or Easter. They have their own festivals and are interested in ours. If you do so, you should not just expect them to turn up. Arrange to meet them or call for them. Realise that they will find a Christian service strange and explain it carefully. Afterwards introduce them to your minister and other church members. A cup of tea at this point will help them to feel more at home.

Public meetings

Again you should not invite Hindu friends to Christian rallies or evangelistic meetings before you have established a relationship of trust with them. Explain beforehand the sort of things that are likely to happen. If a speaker invites people to go forward to receive Christ do not press your

friends to do so. When Hindus are urged to raise
their hands in such meetings, go forward or sign
decision cards, they may react with suspicion
thinking these are pressure tactics to force them to
become Christians. By themselves, these methods
are not wrong but you must explain beforehand
why they are being used. It is, however, better to
leave a Hindu to decide for herself.

The use of testimonies
Hindu friends will be interested to know how you
came to faith in Christ. It may be the first time
they realise that Christianity is not a matter of
being born in a Christian family or country but of
personal decision.

Using testimonies of former Hindus who have
become Christians must be done with care. If
one is given in a public meeting or written in
an evangelistic magazine or tract, Hindus may
view it with suspicion, accusing Christians of
propaganda. A discussion with a disciple, one to
one, where questions can be asked and answered
may be more helpful.

Because of the diverse nature of Hinduism no
Hindu can be truly representative of it. A disciple's
view of her former faith is therefore partial, so her
testimony may not attract other Hindus whose
experience is different. However it can be very
useful as an encouragement to Christians who
are concerned about reaching Hindus for Christ.

Follow up
If a Hindu friend makes a profession of faith she
will continue to need a great deal of help. Spend
time with her explaining any matters of Christian

belief that are still new to her. Let her talk to
you about any difficulties she finds in being a
Christian. Join her in secular activities too. In
short be a real friend. Pages 122 and 144. explain
how difficult it may be at first for her to appreciate Christian worship. Explain why Christians
worship as they do and encourage her to keep
on coming to church, arranging to meet her and
accompany her the first few times. If you cannot
do this introduce her to other church members who
can. Joining a house group or Christian cell will
enable her to make friends with other Christians
too. If your church does not have any other members from the same background as herself, help
her to find a group of South Asian Christians who
meet in your locality. If you do not know of one ask
South Asian Concern to help. Worshipping with
them sometimes may help her feel less isolated.
Pages 120 to 121 explain the cost of becoming
a Christian for many Hindus. Some Christians
from a Hindu background find it helpful to meet
with others who have stepped out of one faith
into another. If they are being persecuted by their
family or former religious community or have been
thrown out of their home they can talk with others
who understand their situation. This is not to suggest that they form cliques. But they do need the
support and understanding of Christians of their
own cultural and religious background. They will
have been in the same situation themselves and
can give support in a way that no on else can. This
should not replace membership of a local church.
It is the only community in which a disciple can
be nourished in the word of God, grow in faith
and Christian understanding, and eventually find

security. All church members should be encouraged to help him or her reach this goal.

Whatever 'methods' you use in witnessing to a Hindu pray daily for the Holy Spirit to open her heart to the truth. The Holy Spirit will also help you to share your faith in trust, love and humility. These should characterise of all you do and say.

Things to do

1. Learn the Bible verses suggested in this chapter for witnessing to Hindus. Try to use some of them when you next talk to a Hindu about your Christian faith.

2. If your church does not have any gospels in South Asian languages ask your minister to obtain some (see the address list at the end of the book). Then ask a Christian friend to join you in some door-to-door visiting where you can distribute them. If you cannot recognise the different languages, take a selection. When someone is interested offer her several and let her select the one she reads.

3. Try to find some church members who enjoy drama and practise acting a Bible story which you can perform. Include former Hindus in the cast if possible. Invite friends, especially Hindus, to watch its presentation.

4. Hold an evangelistic prayer meeting, inviting interested Hindus.

5. Do a book swap with a Hindu friend. Give him a gospel, or Christian biography to read and take

some of his literature in return. Prayerfully read this material. It will give you an insight into how Hindus approach spiritual matters. Get hold of Sai Baba's *Man of Miracles* if you can.

6. Pray with your Hindu friend for any special needs in his family.

7. Get the names of family members closest to your Hindu friend and pray for them regularly.

8. Encourage Asian Christians from a particular family group to meet regularly for praise and prayer, though not as a substitute for belonging to a local church. Suggest they ask members of their non-Christian family to come along. The latter will usually be attracted to attend in a non-threatening environment.

THIRTEEN

THE GOSPEL FROM HINDU VIEWPOINTS

Hindus are often upright and proud people, reluctant to take charity from anyone. Presenting the gospel in a way that smacks of charity is a method predestined to fail. Asians hate being in debt. They take pride in paying their bills promptly and in full, and thinking and pondering ways to pay debts is a common Asian preoccupation. In Sanjeev's community, when one Asian sees another Asian sitting in thought he may say, 'What hundi (hoondee) do you have to pay that you look so worried?'. A hundi is a bill of exchange or an IOU.

'I must pay for everything,' think most Hindus. Thus they believe that they will have to pay their karmic debt themselves over thousands of lifetimes. Christians need to convey to them the truth that, no matter how long they worry and ponder, there is no way he or she will manage to pay the hundi of their accumulated sin or karma. The only one who could pay the debt – the supreme God himself – has paid it and has written 'Paid in full' across the bottom of the bill. If the Hindu owned the whole universe, it wouldn't be enough to pay the hundi; the Creator of the universe has given his very self. When a Hindu realises this he feels a huge burden lifted from him.

For Sanjeev, a Hindu trader, this worry about how the weight of his sins could be paid for used to keep him awake night after night. It was a tremendous relief to hear the good news of Christ's payment, once for all, for all his sins.

Only God can pay the wages of sin. This, perhaps, is the very heart of the gospel from a Hindu viewpoint. It is upon the work of Christ that we must concentrate when sharing the gospel with Hindus.

Hindus who become Christians are attracted to Christ for different reasons. If you find a friend drawn to one particular aspect of Jesus' life or work make sure you understand it yourself so that you can talk about it together. Here are some which deserve attention.

The logic of the gospel

Intellectual Hindus usually appreciate a clear presentation of the fundamentals of the Christian faith. Some come to Christ through reading the Bible on their own, without needing it explained by anyone. Romans chapters 1-8 have been particularly convincing to a number of them. One former Hindu tells how he read it daily, chapter by chapter. He was drawn to Paul's logical explanation of the nature of sin and how God delivered men and women from it through his Son, Jesus. One evening he felt himself in God's presence. After finishing the chapter he says, 'I felt clean.

My burden of sin was lifted. I felt gladness and joy in my heart. God had met me.'

Conviction of sin

Some non-intellectual Hindus are convicted when they hear a person speak about sin. They are aware of their own shortcomings and know that they must suffer for their misdeeds, their karma. They believe that there is no escape from that. Having established the fact that their sins cut them off from God, you need to go on to show them that the only answer lies in Jesus.

What happens after death

Hindus have no certainty about what will happen to them after death. They expect to be reborn in another body but are not sure what form this will take. Will the sum total of their karma mean they will be born higher up the scale or further down, maybe even as an animal? This uncertainty can create a lot of anxiety. In contrast Christ promises a certain future after death – eternal life to all his disciples.

Knowing God

When Hindus visit a temple most of them want a darshan, an opportunity to see the image. This is usually kept in an inner shrine. They believe this is the nearest they can get to seeing God. But many Hindus have a deeper longing to know God himself. You may be able to give them copies of John's gospel which tells us we can meet God in Jesus. 'In the beginning was the Word, and the Word was with God, and the Word was God' John(1: 1). When we have made it clear that 'the Word' refers to Jesus we can ask them to read the rest of the gospel and see how he reveals the character of God. We can also show them that Jesus points to God as 'the Father'. This is a revolutionary idea for a Hindu who has been taught that Brahman is an impersonal force.

Union with God

Most Hindus believe that after thousands of rebirths they will eventually be united with Brahman. But they take this to mean that they will lose their personal identity and be merged into him/it. You can show them that their longing for oneness with God can be met in Jesus. We don't become a drop in the ocean but an individual, transformed person, lost in the wonder of God's presence. Go on to explain about the Holy Spirit, who can purify our atman and liberate us to be with God.

Christ the Guru

Hindus believe the best way to come close to Brahman is to become the disciple of a guru, someone experienced in ways of achieving this.

They look to him as their guide. You can point to Jesus as the eternal Guru, referred to in Hindi as the Sanatan Sat Guru Jesu Masih. The experience and knowledge of all human gurus is imperfect. Jesus is the perfect Guru because he is the Son of God. When we become his disciples we can be absolutely sure he is leading us in the right way. No other human guru, however experienced, can give us this certainty.

Christ the healer

Hindus believe that suffering is a result of their karma. A person who is handicapped by sickness, disability or poverty is only reaping the consequences of wrong behaviour in a previous life, and so it is their own fault. Ask a Hindu friend to read the healing miracles of Jesus. This revelation of God's compassion for human beings will probably be a new thought and may well move him deeply. Many Hindus are attracted to Jesus by this aspect of his ministry. They are also drawn to human beings who have a ministry of healing.

Christ the liberator

There is much that binds the Hindu; for example, the caste system in Hinduism means that a person is bound to the caste into which he has been born. If a man's father is a brahmin his son will be a brahmin too. If a man belongs to a low caste he will be considered inferior by Hindus of a higher caste and so will his son. The dowry system, which means a man must pay a large sum of money to his future son-in-law's family, sometimes results in a bride's father incurring debts that it may take him a lifetime to pay off. Indeed such debts are sometimes passed down from one generation to another. But the debt we owe God has been paid off by Jesus.

Jesus appeals to low caste Hindus because he promises, 'The Spirit of the Lord is upon me, because he has chosen me to bring good news to the poor. He has sent me to proclaim liberty to the captives and recovery of sight to the blind; to set free the oppressed and announce that the time has come when the Lord will save his people' (Luke 4: 18–19).

Christ versus rituals

A Hindu's life is governed by numerous rituals which he has to perform at every stage of life as well as in its daily routine (see chapters three to six). Any omission damages his karma. You can tell him the truth that God is interested in the attitude of a man's heart, rather than how well he performs religious rituals.

Some Hindus are aware that, though they recite prayers, perform sacrifices, fast regularly and observe other ascetic practices, they receive no response from God. They may begin to feel that these acts are empty and futile. You can share Colossians 2:13–14 with a Hindu friend:

You were at one time spiritually dead because of your sins and because you were

Gentiles without the Law. But God has
now brought you to life with Christ. God
forgave us all our sins; he cancelled the
unfavourable record of our debts with
its binding rules and did away with it
completely by nailing it to the cross.

Share with him, too, how you experience the presence of Jesus in your daily life. And tell him about
the ways God has answered your prayers, guided
you and protected you from danger.

Christ the ideal man

Many of the Hindu sacrifices can only be performed by a priest. Without him Hindus believe
the gods won't accept them. But the Hindu priest
is also a sinful human being. So worshippers
have no certainty that God will accept even his
sacrifices. They also have to offer them over and
over again. Many do so every day. Jesus was a
man too, but the one perfect man without sins or
shortcomings. He offered the perfect sacrifice, once
for all, for the sins of all human beings. Because of
this, Christians can come directly to God without
needing a go-between. Sunil is another Asian who
made the change from being a Hindu to being a
follower of Christ, the perfect role model:

Sunil's story

Although I was born in India I came to
England with my parents at the age of

two and a half. As a young child my only
contact with Christianity was through
school assemblies and hymn singing,
practically none of which I recall now.

I tended to think, like most of my Asian
contemporaries, that England and all
English people were Christian. Hence all
aspects of English culture – low moral
values in the media and films, the high
divorce rate, football hooligans etc. were a
reflection of Christianity.

In contrast I had my Hindu and Indian
origins. I didn't really understand what
that meant, but felt proud to be part of
a culture dating back many thousands of
years. Going back to India every few years
made me sense that something was there
which the West lacked.

However I had to admit there was a
certain tension within me. I knew I wasn't
English but then neither was I Indian. I felt
I was stuck in some halfway situation. With
such thoughts as these I started to study
medicine. Within a short space of time my
world seemed to fall apart. I found myself
surrounded almost entirely by English
people. I tried to make friends with some
of them, but there seemed to be such a gulf
between what I expected of friendship and
what they expected.

I remember that time as a period of
intense searching. I was desperately looking
for something solid to my life. I tried to
copy my contemporaries and live basically
to enjoy myself. This included late night

parties and extensive socialising. But it
didn't fill the growing emptiness in my life.
I tried being busy and getting very involved
with sports. But nothing I did ever seemed
enough.

I knew a few Christians at university
but I felt they were arrogant, describing
Christianity as 'the only way' and that they
were only interested in converting people
to their religion. However it did seem
strange to me that young people should
be so 'religious'. I had to admit that they
appeared to have higher moral standards
than other English people I knew.

I found within me a hunger to seek God.
Nothing else in this life appeared able
to satisfy me. I didn't discuss this with
Christians, though, because I thought
they'd try to 'convert' me. I didn't want
to be persuaded by human arguments.
I decided I would seek for the God who
created me and the whole world.

As I was from Hinduism, that's where
I started – chanting prayers, learning
about inner peace. I learnt from Hinduism
that drawing near to God was about inner
meditation and doing good. Yet within me
I knew there were all sorts of thoughts and
feelings which were wrong.

I decided to look at other religions, but,
again, I would do this without telling
anyone. I found some Christian books
on prayer and was quickly challenged by
them. They talked of prayer as being open
and honest with God, telling him exactly

how you felt. I'd never come across such concepts before and they made a deep impression on me. As I began to learn more about this type of prayer, I found God lifted me out of my depression. I knew that it was not me, but God's power. I started to spend several hours of the day trying to pray and reach out to God.

I spoke to some committed Christians, being careful not to appear too interested, in case they tried to convert me. One of them made a comment, that becoming a Christian was a commitment you made in your heart. What was important was your inner self and where that was with respect to God. The comment was only made as an aside, but it made a deep impression on me.

I came to the conclusion that if that was what a Christian was, then I too would follow Jesus. I had so many questions in my mind, so much I didn't understand, but it appeared to be the only way I could go. So I prayed alone, with much fear and trembling.

I gradually told a few Christians whom I felt I could trust and I also started to read the Bible – a book I knew practically nothing about. The effect this had on me I can only describe as 'it blew my mind'. I was struck by the life and commitment of Jesus. Paul's letters also spoke deeply to me, as he shared about his inner struggle against sin and 'I don't do the good I want to do; instead, I do the evil that I do not want to do' (Romans 7: 19). I also felt a

great sense of empathy with the characters
mentioned in 1 Peter who were 'aliens and
strangers on earth', being myself neither
Indian nor British.

I didn't feel at that stage that I could
share my commitment with my family. I
knew their reaction would be total horror.
I asked the Lord to show me more of the
reality of Hinduism first. Soon the way
opened for me to go to India.

I went to various Hindu temples and read
some books on Hinduism, comparing it all
with the Bible. As I did this, it was as if
a fire was growing stronger and stronger
within me that the Bible was *the* truth.

When I returned to England I found I
could no longer contain myself and told my
family of my commitment. As I feared, they
were appalled. They took it as a personal
rejection of themselves, thinking I would
forget them, change my name, and become
'English'. They felt I'd been 'brain-washed'.
Human discussion proved hopeless.

I also had difficulties with other
Christians. The Bible told me they were
now my brothers and sisters, but on a
cultural level I still found it very difficult
to relate. It was at that stage that the Lord
blessed me by introducing me to the Asian
Christian Fellowship in my city. I met
other Christians with a similar background
to myself and was greatly encouraged by
experiencing growing as a Christian in a
cultural environment in which I could relate
better.

Since then a lot has happened. I'm now married to a lovely Christian girl from England – something if you'd told me ten years earlier I'd never have believed. I'm working in psychiatry.

We continue to pray for my family - it's been eight years since I made my commitment. But we trust in the God who can do far more abundantly than all we can, ask, think or imagine.

Things to Do

1. Think through the basic facts about the Christian faith which you feel Hindus needs to know. Write a summary you can share with them. This shouldn't take longer than five minutes to tell.

2. Ask a Hindu friend to tell you what he finds most attractive about the Christian message. Then share with him what is most attractive to you.

3. Try to find out if there are Christians from a Hindu background in your area. If they are finding it hard to stand for Christ against Hindu relatives and friends give them all the encouragement and practical support you can.

4. Work alongside Asian Christians in your area. Ask them for their advice on sharing the gospel e.g. What appeals to them about Christ.

NOTES

Introduction

1. Britannica World Data, 1991, based on figures for 88 countries.
2. Britain 1992, official handbook of the Central Office of Information.
3. Report on the 1991 census, South Asian Concern with Dawn 2000.

Chapter 2 Making Hindu Friends

1. Roger Hooker and Christopher Lamb, *Love the Stranger* London SPCK, 1986) page 14.

Chapter 3 Beliefs common to most Hindus

1. Swami Yogeshananda, *The Way of the Hindu* (Amersham, Hulton Educational Publications Limited, 1980) page 19.
2. John Bowker, *Worlds of Faith* (B. B. C. 1983) page 165.
3. Swami Yogeshananda, *The Way of the Hindu* page 37.
4. Rabindranath Maharaj, *Death of a Guru*

Chapter 4 Caste, Life Cycle Rituals and Stages of Life

1. John Bowker, *Worlds of Faith* (B.B.C. 1983) page 193.

2. Ram, Gidoomal, with Mike Fearon, *Sari 'n Chips* (Tunbridge Wells, Monarch, 1993).

Chapter 5 Hindu Prayer and Worship.

1. John Bowker, *Worlds of Faith* (B.B.C. 1993) page 108.
2. ibid. page 149.
3. V. P. (Hemant) Kanitkar, *We are Hindus* (Edinburgh, Saint Andrew Press, 1987) page 108.

Chapter 7 The Hindu Scriptures

1. Swami Yogeshananda, *The Way of the Hindu* (Hulton Educational Publications 1980) page 39.
2. John Bowker, *Worlds of Faith* (B.B.C. 1983) page 131.
3. ibid Page 131.
4. ibid Page 131.
5. ibid Page 132.

Chapter 8 Hindu sects and Philosophies

1. Vishal Mangalwadi, *The World of Gurus* (India, Vikas Publishing House PVT Ltd., 1977) page 113.

Chapter 9 Hinduism in Britain

1. Indian High Commission, London 1992.
2. *An Introduction to The World's Oldest Religion*, National Council of Hindu Temples (U.K.) Leicester 1983, letter on inside cover.

GLOSSARY

ahimsa	non-violence
arati	worship ceremony with lights
atman	the soul
bhakti	loving devotion
Brahman	the supreme spirit or ultimate reality
brahmin	member of the highest Hindu caste
dharma	duty
ghee	clarified butter
Gita	short for Bhagavadgita, the most revered of the Hindu scriptures
guru	spiritual teacher
jati	caste
karma	works
moksha	salvation
Om	sacred sound at beginning of prayer
prasad	special food, blessed by the priest and given to worshippers. Also means sacrifice
puja	worship of the gods
samsara	reincarnation
Sanskrit	ancient classical Indian language
satsang	religious gathering
varna	one of the original four castes
yoga	path to salvation

BOOK LIST

Asians in Britain, *Caring for Hindus and their Families*, National Extension College, 1983.

Bridger, Peter, *A Hindu Family in Britain*, Religious Education Press, 1980.

Brooke, Tal, *Lord of the Air*, Delhi, India, Vikas Press,

Burnett, David, *The Spirit of Hinduism*, London, Monarch, 1992.

Celebration of Faith, booklet available from the Evangelical Alliance, London.

Chapman, Colin, *The Christian Message in a Multi-Faith Society*, Latimer House, 1992.

Cole, W. Owen, *Meeting Hinduism*, Harlow, Longman, 1987.

Dodhia, Hitesh K, *Crossing the Cultures*, Grove Books, 1990.

Evangelical Christians for Racial Justice (ed), *Time to Speak* – obtainable from editors.

Ewan, John, *Understanding your Hindu Neighbour*, Lutterworth, 1983.

Gidoomal, Ram, *Sari 'n' Chips*, Tunbridge Wells, Monarch, 1993.

Gidoomal, Ram and Fearon, Mike, *Karma 'n' Chips*, London, Wimbledon Publishing, 1994.

Goldsmith, Martin and Harley, Rosemary, *Who is my Neighbour?*, London, Scripture Union, 1988.

Jackson, Robert, *Religion through Festivals*, Harlow, Longman, 1989.

Kanitkar, V P (Hemant), *We are Hindus*, Saint Andrew Press, 1987. *Hinduism* Cheltenham, Stanley Thornes and Hulton, 1989.

Penney, Sue, *Discovering Religions: Hinduism*, Heinemann Educational, 1990.

National Council of Hindu Temples (U.K.) *Hinduism*, 1983.

Sookhdeo, Patrick (ed), *Sharing Good News*, London, Scripture Union, 1991.

Yogeshananda, Swami *The Way of the Hindu*, Hulton Educational, 1980.

Biographies

Maharaj, Rabindranath, *Death of a Guru*, London, Hodder and Stoughton, 1986.

Menon, Vijay, Found By God, Marshall, 1982.

Sheikh, Bilquis, *I Dared to Call Him Father*, Carlisle, STL, 1978.

Szandoroski, Barbara, *Escape from the Guru*, Marc, 1991.

USEFUL ADDRESSES

Alliance of Asian Christians, Carrs Lane Church Centre, Birmingham, B4 7SX

Asian Christian Outreach, 114 St Mary Street, Southampton, Hants S01 1PF

Association of Christian Teachers, 2 Romeland Hill, St Albans, Herts AL3 4ET

Bible Society, Stonehill Green, Westlea, Swindon, Wilts SN5 7DG

Church Missionary Society, 157 Waterloo Road, London SE1 8VV

CLC Asian Books, 51 The Dean, Alresford, Hants SO24 9BJ

Commission for Racial Equality, Elliot House, 10-12 Allington Street, London SW1

Crosslinks, 251 Lewisham Way, London SE4 1X

Evangelical Christians for Racial Justice, 269 Roltol Park Road, Birmingham B16 0LD

Home Office (Immigration Department and Nationality Department), Lunar House, Wellesley Road, Croydon, Surrey CR9 2BY

In Contact Ministries, St Andrew's Road, Plaistow, London E13 8QD. Slides/films strips on Hinduism.

Indian High Commision, India House, Aldwych, London WC2

INTERSERVE, 325 Kennington Road, London, SE11 4QH. *Through their eyes*, a video pack.

Joint Council for the Welfare of Immigrants, 115 Old Street, London, EC1

Kitab, PO Box 175, Sheffield S11 8EN

Language Recordings International, Unit 20, Moorlands Trading Estate, Bristol Road, Gloucester GL1 5RS

NW Resources Centre, C/O Canon Wilfred Gash, St Pauls Rectory, 174 Chorley New Road, Bolton BL1 4PF

Qalam Projects, 10 Grosvener Road, Hounslow, Middlesex TW3 3ER

St Andrew's Bookshop, St Andrew's Road, Plaistow, London E13 8QD

Scripture Gift Mission, Radstock House, 3 Eccleston Street, London SW1W 9LZ

SIM (UK), Ullswater Crescent, Coulsdon, Surrey CR5 2HR

South Asian Concern, PO Box 43, Sutton, Surrey SM2 5WL

The Council of Churches for Britain and Ireland's Committee for Relations with People of Other Faiths, 2 Eaton Gate, London SW1W 9BL.